Theoretical Evolutions in Person-Centered/Experiential Therapy

Theoretical Evolutions in Person-Centered/Experiential Therapy

APPLICATIONS TO SCHIZOPHRENIC AND RETARDED PSYCHOSES

Garry Prouty

Foreword by LUC ROELENS

PRAEGER

Westport, Connecticut
London

Library of Congress Cataloging-in-Publication Data

Prouty, Garry.
    Theoretical evolutions in person-centered/experiential therapy :
applications to schizophrenic and retarded psychoses / Garry Prouty
; foreword by Luc Roelens.
      p. cm.
    Includes bibliographical references and index.
    ISBN 0–275–94543–X (alk. paper)
    1. Psychoses—Treatment. 2. Psychotherapist and patient.
3. Schizophrenia—Treatment. 4. Mentally handicapped—Mental
health. 5. Client-centered psychotherapy. 6. Existential
psychology. 7. Therapeutic alliance. 8. Interpersonal
communication. I. Title.
RC512.P68 1994
616.89′8—dc20   93–42143

British Library Cataloguing in Publication Data is available.

Library of Congress Catalog Card Number: 93–42143
ISBN: 0–275–94543–X

First published in 1994

Praeger Publishers, 88 Post Road West, Westport, CT 06881
An imprint of Greenwood Publishing Group, Inc.

Printed in the United States of America

The paper used in this book complies with the
Permanent Paper Standard issued by the National
Information Standards Organization (Z39.48–1984).

10 9 8 7 6 5 4 3 2

Copyright Acknowledgments

The author and publisher gratefully acknowledge permission to quote from the following sources:

G. Prouty and M. Kubiak, "The Development of Communicative Contact with a Catatonic Schizophrenic." *Journal of Communication Therapy* 4(1) (1988): 13–20. By permission of the editors.

G. Prouty and M. Kubiak, "Pre-Therapy with Mentally Retarded/Psychotic Clients." *Psychiatric Aspects of Mental Retardation Reviews* 7(10) (1988): 63–64. By permission of Anne D. Hurley.

G. Prouty and M. A. Cronwall, "Psychotherapy with a Depressed Mentally Retarded Adult: An Application of Pre-Therapy." In Anton Dosen et al. (Eds.), *Depression in Mentally Retarded Children and Adults*. Leiden, The Netherlands: Logon Publications, 1990. By permission of Logon Publications.

G. Prouty, "The Pre-Symbolic Structure and Processing of Schizophrenic Hallucinations: The Problematic of a Non-Process Structure." In Lois Fusek (Ed.), *New Directions in Client-Centered Therapy Practice with Difficult Client Populations*. Spring Lecture Series. Chicago: Chicago Counseling and Psychotherapy Research Center, 1991. By permission of the Chicago Counseling and Psychotherapy Research Center.

G. Prouty and S. Pietrzak, "Pre-Therapy Method Applied to Persons Experiencing Hallucinatory Images." *Person-Centered Review* 3(4) (1988): 426–41. By permission of David Cain.

G. Prouty, "Hallucinatory Contact: A Phenomenological Treatment of Schizophrenia." *Journal of Communication Therapy* 2(1) (1983): 99–103. By permission of the editors.

To my brother, Robert Knickerbocker

Contents

Foreword

By developing Pre-Therapy and Pre-Symbolic processing, Garry Prouty has defined existentially relevant distinctions suited for the interpretation of the incomprehensible communicative behavior of severely withdrawn people. Prouty uses these distinctions to reach severely disturbed patients (autistic and chronic schizophrenics, mentally retarded patients with psychotic symptoms) by way of elementary communication channels. When starting his highly original search for contact with these persons, he probably did not realize that he was also lining up in a respectable tradition. Indeed, Manfred Bleuler (1991: 2–3) witnesses:

Eugene Bleuler's concept of schizophrenic psychoses was based first on his experience between 1886 and 1898 . . . in the "Island Clinic of Rheinau." . . . His main endeavor was to be close to his patients; working with them, playing and walking with them, even organizing dancing parties with them. . . . It was in Rheinau that he realized that schizophrenics could not be "demented."

In fact, Prouty offers a therapeutic systematization of the clinically well-known "rare, but remarkable reversal of profoundly chronic and severe psychotic/deficit states after years of illness"

(McGlashan and Fenton, 1993: 81). Authors like Ciompi (1984, 1991), Koukkou-Lehmann (1987), Strauss (1983, 1991), Stromgren (1991), Tienari (1991), and many others point to the dependency of many symptoms of schizophrenia on the environmental and situational context. Given sufficient clinical experience, every psychiatrist will observe the corresponding phenomena.

Stromgren (1991: 39–40), presents two interesting case vignettes. One concerns a farmer's wife. She immediately recovered from a chronic and severe catatonic state upon receiving the message that her husband had fallen down from a roof and broken both legs. Her intention "to go home to take care of everything there" was strong enough to dispel the thought disorders and the defective behavior. Occasional follow-ups after four and ten years revealed that she functioned as an efficient housewife, displaying a mild degree of autism. The other case also illustrates the central role of subjective interpretation and personal motivation in pathological behavior and in spontaneous recovery. To Stromgren, these "two cases demonstrate how "long-lasting, completely incapacitating catatonic symptoms can both originate and again cease as a consequence of delusional misinterpretations of facts" (p. 41). A more therapeutic perspective on the phenomenon of rapid shift from dysfunction to function is taken by Strauss (1991: 82), who infers from other examples: "[W]e need to think about the role of personal meaning in helping to govern the process of shifting from function to dysfunction" (p. 83).

Several years ago, I was confronted with an event that dramatically illustrated the fundamental role of the patient's subjective appreciation. A sixty-year-old chronic schizophrenic had slipped into a dementia-like state. For weeks he was unable to speak, he had to be fed by the nurses, and he had lost control of his sphincter. One day, a nurse offered him a Coke. He choked, coughed, and in doing so, emitted a cloud of droplets of Coke that hit her face. Visibly startled, he immediately and clearly said "Excuse me, I did not intend to do that." Before the nurse was able to answer him, he had sunk again into a dementia-like state and resumed the continuous groaning with which it was impossible to interact.

How can one explain this flashing change of the clinical picture in traditional medical terms of illness?

Many leading authors in the field of schizophrenia are uncomfortable with concepts of schizophrenia as a classical medical illness. Carpenter (1983) stated: "Schizophrenia denotes a disease entity and connotes a human experience. It is difficult to present definitions and concepts which do justice to the disease and the person simultaneously."

Strauss (1991: 86) argues:

Schizophrenia, in its context, is not pure abnormality. It is the coexistence of disorder and order, of abnormal and normal. Viewed from this contextual perspective, the manifestations of schizophrenia reflect the interplay of cognition, feeling and perception, and the way this interplay shifts in situations of comfort, repose, trust, perceived danger and terror.

A growing trend in the literature characterized schizophrenia as a poly-etiological syndrome with many possible arrangements of symptoms. Fruitful research of the last decades indicates that it is sensible to interpret this syndrome in terms of interacting dimensions. Many results of narrowly focused, highly specialized research can be ordered in this frame of reference. They converge on a picture of schizophrenia as a tragic "condition humane," the intermittent or continuous clinical appearance of which is facilitated by a multitude of lesions and pathological mechanisms.

Ciompi (1984) draws a clear picture, in which he discerns:

1. A vulnerable premorbid personality structure, which appears as the final result of complex lifelong interactions between the biological substrate and the total input of psychosocial information. Deficiencies (be it at the genetic, neurobiological, psychophysiological, neuropsychological or psychological level) in the structure of the acquired internal programs, developed to cope with incoming information, will induce difficulties in information processing and reduce the level of stress tolerance. At the levels of psychophysiology and cerebral information-processing, sophisticated research is examining clinically subtle deficits and abnormalities (Nuechterlein et al., 1992; Corcoran and Frith, 1993; O'Carroll, 1992).

2. Acute episodes with visible psychotic symptoms. The appearance of these episodes can be understood as the result of a critical overtaxing of a vulnerable information-processing system. Ciompi understands psychotic patterns of thinking, feeling, and behaving as pathological

new states of equilibrium, reached by a vulnerable information-processing system under the effect of critical overstimulation. At the psychophysiological level, Koukkou-Lehmann (1987) corroborates this perspective by observing differences in information-induced electroencephalographic changes among acute schizophrenic patients, former schizophrenic patients, neurotic patients, and normal controls.

3. A chronic phase that eventually occurs. Concerning the outcome of an acute schizophrenic episode, Benjamin's (1993: 7) considerations are essential:

Attachment, or security, is a vital need. Primates have evolved as group animals, and bonding to the group is essential for survival. . . . If the acts of nurturance and trust that have been programmed in the genetic make-up of the species do not or cannot take place, attachment atrophies or assumes a deviant form.

After an acute episode, the odds are that the recovering patient with his vulnerable and injured personality will be confronted with problems or even handicaps in realizing a satisfying and effective level of functioning. The availability or the absence of suitable ways of "containment" can be tremendously important in regard to the long-term effects of the way the acute schizophrenic crisis is resolved. Mundt (1990: 41) hypothesizes that the schizophrenic "defect state acts as a balance between restricted intentionality and the maintenance of some bridge of reciprocity (for as much traffic as the bridge can bear)." Prouty demonstrates that it is possible to search for personal contact while alleviating the burden of confrontation for the patient. The use of Pre-Therapy and Pre-Symbolic processing leads to a Client-Centered elaboration of containment, in which better levels of reciprocity can unfold.

In discussing the mechanisms involved in the development of the clinical syndrome, insufficient attention is given to the fact that even normal mechanisms can play a pathogenetic role by producing long-lasting deadlocking effects. Tustin (1992) reports clinical evidence of the psychogenic origin of some forms of childhood autism. Stromgren (1991) considers autism to be at the core of the schizophrenic reaction. To him, it "is a defense mechanism that is applied when the person experiences intolerable idiosyncratic reactions" (p. 44).

Years ago, one of my patients took a job in a security firm some months after recovering from an acute schizophrenic episode. As a guard, he had to monitor the content of the bags carried by the entering factory workers. One employee was so angered that he called my patient every name in the book. The patient reacted with a catatonic episode that lasted for three hours and faded subsequently.

Research at the neurobiological and neurobiochemical level underpins clinical insights of this kind. Weinberger (1987) reports the finding of Herman, Guilloneau, and Dantzer (1982) that with electric shock, dopamine metabolism increases in both mesolimbic and mesocortical terminal fields. If the animal is returned to the cage, but not shocked, dopamine metabolism still increases in the prefrontal cortex, but does not change elsewhere. Weinberger concludes: "While all dopamine systems respond to visceral stress, the prefrontal afferentation system is uniquely sensitive to experiential stress" (p. 665).

Ljungberg (1987) draws our attention to the observation that mammals may develop different types of aberrant behavior reactions when exposed to severe psychosocial stress. These animals may show long-lasting changes in dopaminergic transmission after severe stress. It has also been found that the behavioral disturbances induced can be diminished by neuroleptical treatment. The effects of the stressor have also been shown to depend on the age of the animal; that is, sensitive periods exist. Individual (genetically determined) differences have been found, and certain stressors have been shown to have more damaging effects than others. Special emphasis has been put on disturbances in social interactions.

Furthermore, Ljungberg (1986) found indications in the literature "that an increased dopaminergic transmission disrupts the ability for selective attention in animals. [T]his effect can be obtained by severe stress." He correctly argues that these findings have implications for the discussion about the role of changes in the dopaminergic transmissions: Are they to be considered as the cause or as the result in schizophrenia and in schizophrenia-like syndromes?

These findings make it clear that even in the neurophysiological dysfunctions a central place must be allotted to the causal role of unbearable psychic burdening. The destructive influence of such burdens, equaling the impact of somatic brain lesions, argues for perspicacity in the development of suitable treatment. Again, the quality of interpersonal bonding is at stake (Benjamin, 1993). These considerations transcend the private level of writing desk fantasies.

Nuechterlein et al. (1992) recently reported on longitudinal studies of vulnerability and stress in schizophrenic disorders. They "confirmed through rigorous prospective methods that stressful life events, independent of the patient's illness and beyond the patient's control, occur with disproportionately high frequency in the months before psychotic exacerbations and relapses" (p. 416). They indicate "that it might be possible to identify signs and symptoms prodromal to psychotic relapses in about 60% of patients during the early period of schizophrenia" (p. 417). Quite an indication that individually tailored interpersonal prevention, even when only modestly effective, could alleviate psychic suffering! Offering a corrective interpersonal alliance to provide a suited context for containment and eventually processing the (possibly idiosyncratic) terrorizing personal experience is not a standard procedure in current psychiatric practice.

Too often, in everyday psychiatry, the treatment of schizophrenia is reduced to influencing the symptoms with neuroleptics. For a large group of patients, neuroleptics indeed force a shift toward the disappearance or weakening of many symptoms and to partial or global recovery of their habitual coping capacities; they are helped considerably by these drugs. But these advantages should not lead to oversimplification of the problem or to ill-considered use. Neuroleptic drugs aim at reducing the activity of the mesocortical and mesolimbic dopamine systems in the brain (Weinberger, 1987). However, their action mechanisms are so complex that they can interfere with other cerebral systems, leading to the well-known extrapyramidal effects and to tardive dyskinesia; they may even produce disturbing behavioral effects (Mayerhoff and Lieberman, 1992). Vast amounts of biochemical and pharmacological research on these drugs have improved this treatment modality and have broadened our knowledge of it. But "yet there is not unequivocal demonstration that increased dopamine activity is at the root of the schizophrenic illness" (Straube and Oades, 1992: 622). Pharmacological treatment continues to be an antisymptomatic approach that often yields impressive results. Under the contemporary economical pressure toward cost-effectiveness of treatment regimes, the risk persists that this treatment modality unjustly continues to outshine the other treatment necessities. In industrialized countries, the personnel needed for optimal "containment" is an expensive factor indeed. But its relative shortage too often provokes ignorance of its effects.

Ciompi (1991: 25) reports "good to satisfactory results in about two-thirds of cases" of acute schizophrenia in the experimental therapeutic setting, Soteria Berne in Switzerland. The use of neuroleptics was restricted. In a series of 51 patients, 20 patients were treated without neuroleptics, most of the other 31 receiving lower doses than is usual in psychiatric practice (Ciompi et al., 1991). Windgassen and Tolle (1991) critically question the general applicability of this approach, referring to arguments about staffing and motivation. But Mundt (1991: 5) points out that schizophrenia has a variable outcome across cultures. If so, the different ways by which "bonding to the group" (Benjamin, 1993) is realized in different cultures, promoting or hampering the process of recovery, have to be unveiled.

Jablensky (1993: 47) reports:

The tendency for schizophrenic patients in "non-Western" cultures to remit earlier, have longer remissions of symptoms and less disability has now been confirmed by the 5-year follow up data of the International Pilot Study of Schizophrenia. This pattern has been replicated in the 1- and 2-year follow up of the World Health Organization ten-country study. . . . [T]he main difference in the course of schizophrenia in the two types of setting was . . . in the significantly higher proportion of patients in the developed countries (57.2% compared with 24.1% in the developing countries) who never achieved a complete remission and were impaired by continuous residual symptoms.

Prouty's contributions could well prove to have relevant remediating value for the culturally unfavorable circumstances in which Western patients have to recover.

Strauss (1991: 89) spells out the context in which Prouty has been working for many years:

The meaning of schizophrenia compared to the person's competent functioning and the linked interactions between competence and dysfunction; this context may be the framework essential for understanding the meaning of schizophrenia and the processes involved in disorder and healing.

Prouty has founded a Client-Centered tradition of attuning to the very limited possibilities of communication of severely withdrawn people. As indicated before, this is a very relevant translation into the field of treatment of the well-known fact that the clinical syndrome of chronic schizophrenia can undergo variations and that it is amongst others dependent on the interpersonal environmental context.

Professionals can be trained in finding Prouty's interpersonal stance toward an autistic or severely withdrawn patient by developing their sensitivity to some of his subtle signals starting from a deep respect for the person the patient is. Applying Prouty's therapeutic techniques from that stance induces changes in some patients that are out of reach of traditional psychiatric care. (Refer to the case vignettes presented by Stromgren, 1991.)

In 1989, Pre-Therapy was introduced to a group of psychiatric nurses and occupational therapists in the mental hospital of Sint-Amandus, Beernem, Belgium. At this writing, three of the five teams involved in the project have documented on videotape changes in "contact behavior" of chronic schizophrenic patients without any possibility of changing their usual work load. Clearly, changes in the interaction with chronic withdrawn patients, offering them opportunities for bonding along Pre-Therapeutic lines, generate shifts in the interpersonal behavior of some of these chronic "worn-out" patients.

I hope that many colleagues and psychiatrists will acknowledge the importance of Prouty's contributions.

Luc Roelens
Sint-Martins-Latem, Belgium
May 1993

REFERENCES

Benjamin, L. S. (1993). Every psychopathology is a gift of love. *Psychotherapy Research*, *3*, 1–24.

Bleuler, M. (1991). The concept of schizophrenia in Europe during the past one hundred years. In Flack, W. F., D. R. Miller, and M. Wiener (eds.). *What Is Schizophrenia?* New York: Springer-Verlag, pp. 1–15.

Carpenter, Jr., W. T. (1983). What is schizophrenia? *Schizophrenia Bulletin*, *9*, 9–10.

Ciompi, L. (1984). Is there really a schizophrenia? The long-term course of psychotic phenomena. *British Journal of Psychiatry*, *145*, 636–40.

———. (1991). Affect logic and schizophrenia. In C. Eggers (ed.). *Schizophrenia and Youth. Etiology and Therapeutic Consequences*. Berlin: Springer-Verlag, pp. 15–27.

Ciompi, L., H. P. Dauwalder, Ch. Maier, and E. Aebi. (1991). Das Pilotprojekt "Soteria Bern" zur Behandlung akut Schizophrneer. I. Konzeptuelle Grundlagen, praktische Realisierung, klinische Erfahrunger. *Nervenarzt, 62*, 428–35.

Corcoran, R., and C. D. Frith. (1993). Neuropsychology and neurophysiology in schizophrenia. *Current Opinion in Psychiatry, 6*, 74–79.

Herman, J. P., D. Guilloneau, and R. Dantzer. (1982). Differential effects of inescapable foot shocks and of stimuli previously paired with inescapable foot shock on dopamine turnover in cortical and limbic areas of the rat. *Life Science, 30*, 2207–14. Cited in Weinberger 1987.

Jablensky, A. (1993). The epidemiology of schizophrenia. *Current Opinion in Psychiatry, 6*, 43–52.

Jones, E. G. (1993). The development of primate neocortex—an overview. In S. A. Mednick, T. D. Cannon, C. E. Barr, and M. Lyon (eds.). *Fetal Neural Development and Adult Schizophrenia*. Cambridge: Cambridge University Press, pp. 40–65.

Koukkou-Lehmann, M. (1987). *Hirnmechanismen normalen und schizophrenen Denkens*. Berlin: Springer-Verlag.

Ljungberg, T. (1986). Personal communication.

———. (1987). The dopamine systems in the brain, functional classification of different dopamine receptors. *Acta Psychiatrica Belgica, 87*, 523–34.

Mayerhoff, D. I., and J. A. Lieberman. (1992). Behavioral effects of neuroleptics. In J. M. Kane and J. A. Lieberman (eds.). *Adverse Effects of Psychotropic Drugs*. New York: Guilford Press.

McGlashan, T. C., and W. S. Fenton. (1993). Subtype progression and pathophysiological deterioration in early schizophrenia. *Schizophrenia Bulletin, 19*, 71–84.

Mednick, S. A., T. D. Cannon, C. E. Barr, and M. Lyon (eds.). (1991). *Fetal Neural Development and Adult Schizophrenia*. Cambridge: Cambridge University Press.

Mundt, Ch. (1990). Concepts of intentionality and their application to the psychopathology of schizophrenia—a critique of the vulnerability-model. In M. Spitzer and B. A. Maher (eds.). *Philosophy and Psychopathology*. New York: Springer-Verlag, pp. 35–43.

———. (1991). Endogenitat von Psychosen—Anachronismus oder aktueller Wegweiser fur die Pathogeneseforshung? *Nervenarzt, 62*, 3–15.

Nuechterlein, K. H., M. E. Dawson, M. Gitlin, J. Ventura, M. J. Goldstein, K. S. Snyder, C. M. Yee, and J. Mintz. (1992). Developmental processes in schizophrenic disorders: Longitudinal studies of vulnerability and stress. *Schizophrenia Bulletin, 18*, 387–425.

O'Carroll, R. (1992). Neuropsychology of psychosis. *Current Opinion in Psychiatry, 5*, 38–44.

Royston, M. C., and S. W. Lewis. (1993). Brain pathology in schizophrenia: developmental or degenerative? *Current Opinion in Psychiatry, 6*, 70–73.

Straube, E. R., and R. D. Oades. (1992). *Schizophrenia, Empirical Research and Findings.* San Diego: Academic Press.

Strauss, J. S. (1983). What is schizophrenia? *Schizophrenia Bulletin, 9*, 7–9.

———. (1991). The meaning of schizophrenia: compared to what? In Flack, W. F., D. R. Miller, and M. Wiener (eds.). *What is Schizophrenia?* New York: Springer-Verlag, pp. 81–90.

Stromgren, E. (1991). Autism: Core of the schizophrenic reaction. In Flack, W. F., D. R. Miller, and M. Wiener (eds.). *What is Schizophrenia?* New York: Springer-Verlag, pp. 33–44.

Tienari, P. (1991). Gene-environment interaction in adoptive families. In Hafner, H. and W. F. Gattaz (eds.). *Search for the Causes of Schizophrenia, Vol. 2.* Berlin: Springer-Verlag, pp. 126–43.

Tustin, F. (1992). *Autistic States in Children.* London: Routledge.

Weinberger, D. R. (1987). Implications of normal brain development for the pathogenesis of schizophrenia. *Archives of General Psychiatry, 44*, 660–69.

Windgassen, K., and R. Tolle. (1991). Wie konnen wir die Schizophrenen besser behandeln? Anmerkunger zu der Arbeit von L. Ciompi, H. P. Dauwalder, Ch. Maier and E. Aebi. *Nervenarzt, 62*, 577–79.

Preface

I have written this book as an expression of my concern for many theoretical and human issues.

The text describes an interpretation of Carl Rogers' theory and its evolution into an Experiential phase through the work of Eugene Gendlin, which has resulted in what is commonly called the Person-Centered/Experiential Movement. One very significant criticism of this body of theory is that its major validity is limited to outpatient, functional, high-level clients. I have attempted to describe theoretical evolutions that will resolve some of the criticism while still maintaining the integrity of the original theories. I hope I have achieved this difficult balance.

Many schizophrenic and psychotic/retarded patients are too regressed, autistic, isolated and "out of contact" for classical psychotherapy. In the United States I have observed these clients in many "back" wards receiving custodial services. They appear to be inaccessible for psychological care. Such clients do not seem to have the capacity for human relatedness. This lack removes the element of communicative hope and thus psychotherapy becomes counter-indicated.

As explained in this book, Pre-Therapy has been developed from the hypothesis that certain psychological functions are necessary for psychotherapy with these clients. The functions are reality, affective, and communicative contact. When these functions are facilitated, psychotherapy can progress. However, realistically, many of these clients aren't capable of introspective affective process. Pre-Therapy accepts this, but still offers hope that reality-appropriate communication can be restored or developed so that clients can function in programmatic services, such as vocational, social, and educational. Consequently, a better quality of life for the clients is developed within the institution.

Another issue of concern in this book is the hallucination. It is conceived of as a fragment of the self. This presents the self as a "divided self"—a psychological problem, but one that is treatable. The successful treatment of hallucinations is a restoration of the self.

In essence, these theoretical and clinical concerns are about restoring a communicative human self that was lost in madness or retardation.

Acknowledgments

This book represents the contributions of many persons and organizations.

First, I would like to acknowledge the mentoring of Dr. Eugene Gendlin, Department of Psychology, University of Chicago. Dr. Gendlin gave freely of his time and energy through endless hours of supportive discussion and clinical supervision. Large portions of the clinical work presented in this book were developed during approximately the first two years of my clinical training. It was Dr. Gendlin's unique encouragement and affirmation during this formative phase that enabled the growth of this work. Through him I learned the essence and spirit of the Person-Centered/Experiential approach to psychotherapy. He was a truly profound teacher.

Among my American colleagues, I would like to extend appreciation to Dr. Bert Karon of Michigan State University for his encouragement relative to the psychotherapy of schizophrenia. He is one of the few American pioneers to steadfastly maintain the value of psychotherapy with this difficult population. I would also like to acknowledge the encouragement of Dr. Steven Reiss, Nisonger Center, Ohio State University, an innovative leader for mental health work with the mentally retarded. In addition, thanks are extended to Dr. Margaret Warner of the Illinois School of Professional Psychology for her early and continued valuing of this approach. Gratitude also is given to Barbara Roy of the Chicago Counseling Center for her use of Pre-Therapy with multiple-personality clients. Special thanks go to Arthur Sondler, colleague and psychotherapist, who gave much early support through hours and hours of "on-site" discussion and evaluation. Dr. Elfie Hinterkopf and Les Brunswick, formerly of Governors State University, gave impetus to early empirical explorations.

Among the people who contribute to a professor's development are his students. I owe special recognition to Sharon Pietrzak, whose extremely hard work was the foundation for the early pilot studies and whose collaboration in publication was invaluable. I also owe special thanks to Mary Ann Kubiak for her collaboration in publishing clinical case histories and much personal support. Recognition also is given to Mindy Cronwall for her clinical work and publishing collaboration. Although these people are all professionals now, their contributions were made during their student years, thereby accenting their talents.

In 1985, the impetus of my work changed to Europe. Dr. Bart Santen extended an invitation to present a week-long seminar in the Netherlands, and a new world of stimulation and collaboration opened. Dion Van Werde of Belgium, a Pre-Therapy Staff Fellow of the Chicago Counseling and Psychotherapy Center, emerged as a principal collaborator. He has written numerous articles on Pre-Therapy and developed the work further to a psychiatric ward model. In addition, he worked endless hours developing workshops and lectures on this approach. Hans Peters, a specialist in mental retardation from the Netherlands, has published considerable work on Pre-Therapy. Mia Leijssen and Dr. Luc Roelens of Belgium published an excellent theoretical description. Additional thanks are due to Dr. Roelens for his exploratory work with Pre-Therapy at St. Amundus Hospital, Beernem, Belgium, and to Prof. Dr. Rik Willemaers of Belgium for his supervision of supportive research. Extra special thanks go to Swiss psychologist Marlis Portner for her support over many years and for her special efforts at publication and translation. Appreciation is expressed to Dr. Alberto Zucconi, who sponsored many workshops throughout Italy, and to Dr. Valeria Vaccari for her introduction of this work to the Italian psychiatric community. Gratitude is also given to Paulo Rossi, who made these workshops successful by translating with deep understanding. Helmuth Beutel is thanked for introducing this work into Germany. Appreciation is also given to Yvonne Badelt of Germany for her introduction of Pre-Therapy to retardation professionals. Deep gratitude is also expressed to Dr. Henrietta Morato of the University of Sao Paulo, Brazil, for expanding the concept of Pre-Therapy to include culturally deprived children.

Returning "home," special recognition and appreciation should be extended to Prairie State College on several levels. Without its cooperation and assistance, much of this book could not have been achieved. Specifically, thanks go to Dr. James Moore, dean of arts and sciences, for his valuing of the total project over a long period of time. Thanks also to Dr. James Tegtmeyer, vice president of academic affairs, and Dr. Timothy Lightfield, president, for their administrative support relative to release time and salary, which made this book possible. Appreciation is also extended to Dr. Michael Greenwich, assistant professor of mathematics and statistics, Purdue University (Calumet) for statistical consultation.

Much appreciation is extended to the Prairie State Foundation, which financially assisted early pilot studies at a local mental health facility. Finally, I am grateful to the Prairie State College board of trustees, whose policies supported these various administrative contributions.

My sincere thanks to all of the following persons who have contributed their time, energy, and skills to the process of editing, typing, reading, and evaluating this book.

Deep respect is accorded Dr. Anton Dosen and Dr. Gert Jan Verberne, both of the Netherlands, for their careful, thoughtful commentary and study of this manuscript.

Gratitude, appreciation, and respect are given to Pamela Reynolds for her dedicated and precise editing of this work.

On a special level, extensive gratitude is given to my secretary, Glenné Benz. Her relentless efforts to produce and develop manuscripts made this text possible. She worked endless hours with true commitment.

On a purely personal basis, much affectionate appreciation is due to Dr. Wim Lucieer of the Netherlands, a psychiatrist who gave many hours of even-handed reading and assessing of this book.

Much gratitude is also expressed for his personal support. He and his wife, Addie, often gave extensively of their warmth and hospitality. He truly introduced me to the humanistic tradition of Dutch psychiatry.

Ultimately, in a way that cannot be fully expressed, I thank my wife, Jill, for her infinite spiritual support and practical assistance.

Introduction

In 1940, Carl Rogers introduced a unique approach to psychotherapy that first became known as "Non-Directive," then "Client-Centered," and finally "Person-Centered." Whatever the label, the treatment had as its key assumption the hypothesis that the client possessed the self-autonomous resources for internal change. Although Rogers did not use this exact language, he hypothesized that the organism had the capacity for "becoming" and that the therapist's function was to facilitate this "becoming." This facilitation occurred best when the therapist was an empathic, accepting, congruent, and non-directive presence. In addition, this facilitation occurred if the therapist was committed to "entering" and "following" the phenomenological "lived experience" of the client.

Because of the validity, simplicity, and clarity of Rogers' views and writings, this new approach became popular among counselors, social workers, psychologists, and others involved in psychological healing. Rogers and his colleagues eventually supported this theory with a considerable amount of research. This work, combined with his writing, resulted in the Person-Centered movement in the United States and other countries.

After the development and validation of his approach to individual therapy, Rogers expanded his application to group therapy, education and inter-cultural conflict. Through this work, Rogers expanded and fulfilled his vision of a general theory of human relationships.

During the 1960s, Eugene Gendlin, a student of Rogers, contributed a major expansion in Person-Centered theory from relationship to experiencing.

Gendlin hypothesized that experiencing was a critical element in therapeutic change. He described experiencing in terms of an organismic phenomenology and developed a specific technique— "focusing"—to facilitate the experiencing. Although Gendlin's and Rogers' theoretical views differ in some respects, both (or elements of both) lead to a Person-Centered/Experiential interpretation of psychotherapy.

Germain Lietaer, the well-known Flemish professor and Client-Centered therapist, described the Wisconsin Study (schizophrenia) as very significant in Person-Centered history. It ended the era of a major locus for theoretical research and the development of Rogers' views. I would like to add that it also is significant because it ended Rogers' involvement with psychiatry. The result was a minimal amount of Person-Centered/Experiential research and therapy with severely impaired clients. This, of course, contributed to the assertion of critics that the Person-Centered/Experiential approach was mostly effective with high-level, functional clients who were not psychiatrically impaired. (A noteworthy exception is the work of Teusch of Germany.) This criticism was further strengthened by Rogers' early view that Person-Centered therapy was not appropriate for mentally retarded clients.

This book is an attempt to resolve the "vacuum" in the Person-Centered/Experiential approach with severely regressed and psychiatrically impaired clients. Its purpose is to describe theoretical and clinical evolutions needed to extend the Person-Centered/Experiential approach to mentally retarded and schizophrenic clients.

Part I of this book is a review and *interpretation* of Rogers' and Gendlin's major theoretical contributions. I have taken the liberty of interpreting each theorist separately and exploring the somewhat controversial theoretical interfaces between the two. Rogers is described in a cultural and historical context and as a relationship theorist. His views are applied in terms of psychotic clients.

Gendlin's theoretical contributions are described during his Client-Centered phase of the late 1950s, 1960s, and the early 1970s. This was the era of his most significant impact on Rogerian therapy and coincided with my period of study with him. This is important because I learned "non-directive experiencing" as contrasted with Gendlin's later, somewhat more directive, "focusing." In other words, my clinical development was more non-directive than that of many of Gendlin's later students. This is reflected in the non-directive approach of Pre-Therapy.

Part II describes the movement from "classical" Rogerian therapy to Pre-Therapy. Rogers is evaluated in terms of his first necessary and sufficient condition of therapy—psychological contact.

Rogers does not describe the nature of psychological contact; neither does he describe any clinical method to assist in its absence. Perls describes psychological contact as an ego function, but also fails to develop this definition. Pre-Therapy, in broad terms, is presented as the development of the psychological functions necessary for psychotherapy: reality, affective, and communicative contact. These, in turn, are described as clinical technique, internal functions and behavioral expressions. In essence, the therapist's "work," the client's "process," and measurable behavioral outcome are delineated. Case histories and pilot studies are also presented.

Part III presents an epistemic shift from the primacy of bodily Experiencing to a symbolic construct—from bodily phenomenology to hallucinatory symbology. Further, it outlines the development of Pre-Symbolic theory and methods. It is a description of the structure of hallucinations and their use in treatment.

The use of hallucinations in treatment is a unique assertion that is predicated on an evolution of Perls' Gestalt therapy. Gestalt therapy describes the dream as a "self-fragment" to be integrated. It is only a step further to assert that the hallucination is a self-fragment to be integrated. The goal of Pre-Symbolic therapy then becomes the integration of a profoundly "divided self."

The Pre-Symbolic structure of a hallucination is analyzed in terms of its symbolic and phenomenological properties. Is the hallucination a symbol or a phenomenon? This question is asked because the two views can be conceived theoretically as opposing logics. Are symbology and phenomenology two different ways to understand the hallucination? They are both present in the structure of the hallucination. What does this mean in definitional terms? The resolution of these questions results in the formation of the conceptual form "Pre-Symbolics."

The implications of Pre-Symbolic theory for Person-Centered and Experiential theory are examined. The contrasting modes of self-experiencing between the hallucinating psychotic and Rogers' "fully functioning person" are presented. The necessity of redefining classical Experiential theory to include Pre-Symbolic Experiencing is explored.

Pre-Symbolic Process I, II, III, and IV are described as clinical methods. Although differing in technique, these methods have in common the integration and processing of the hallucinatory experience.

Part I

HISTORICAL FOUNDATIONS

Chapter 1

Carl Rogers: An Interpretation

THE NON-DIRECTIVE ATTITUDE

Carl Rogers' theory of psychotherapy is presented as a set of therapist "core attitudes" (Mearns and Thorne, 1990) that help facilitate the self-actualizing or self-formative tendency of the organism (Rogers, 1963, 1978). Classically, these core attitudes are articulated as unconditional positive regard (UCPR), empathy, and congruence (Rogers, 1959). While certainly characterizing the Rogerian working model of psychotherapy, this description does not fully convey the historical-revolutionary aspect of Rogers' therapeutic thought.

To frame Rogers historically is to understand him as part of Protestant culture (Van Belle, 1980). Rogers' views can be interpreted as a form of Protestant individualism, as illustrated by comparing Martin Luther and Rogers. Luther's theology individualizes moral conscience above the Church—between man and deity, beyond the social form to God. Luther, in this theological concept, shifted the power to define moral reality from the social to the individual. Moral conscience becomes a form of self-empowerment.

Rogers, in this century, paralleled Luther. He developed a form of psychotherapy in which individuals are conceived of as having the internal resources to define and process their own psychological reality. The power to define one's own psychological being is transferred from the therapist to the client. The power to define psychological meaning moved from the social form to the individual client. Rogers himself (1977) realized this revolutionary act in terms of the field of mental health, but failed to recognize the larger historical comparison. Luther empowered individuals to define their moral reality; Rogers empowered individuals to define their psychological reality. In both instances, the person individuates. This is the Protestant ethos—individualization.

How does Rogers carry this thrust of individualization into psychotherapy? It is brought to therapy by what can be labeled the "non-directive attitude."[1]

Very definitely, Rogers does not include a non-directive attitude among the core attitudes for therapy; yet it is present in Rogers' work from the inception. Initially, Rogers (1942) conceived non-directiveness as a concrete style of therapist response: The client is described as taking responsibility for directing the interview. The counselor responds in such a way as to indicate recognition of preceding messages. The counselor responds to the client's immediate feeling and attitude. The counselor indicates that the decision is up to the client and indicates acceptance of the client's decision.

Rogers, then, abstracts non-directiveness to a set of values to be held by the counselor: The client has the right to select individual goals. The client has the right to be psychologically independent and to maintain psychological integrity. The client has the right to choose the best reality adaptation.

In terms of therapy practice, it can be added that the counselor does not guide, direct, interpret, explain, or advise the client. His or her primary responsibility is to follow and facilitate the client's process.

In more modern Person-Centered language, the client is self-empowered in the therapy session. The client's autonomy is maximized, the therapeutic relationship is more democratized and the client's individualization is more centered. In alternate language, the client is psychologically liberated to become a self.[2]

It seems obvious that in order to implement this non-directive approach, the counselor must have a genuine and congruent non-directive attitude. Implicitly or explicitly, the therapist needs to value human freedom. This attitude greatly respects and accepts human autonomy and self-empowerment. Such an attitude also welcomes democratized relationships in which power agendas are minimized. This attitude includes the conviction that clients have the right and the capacity to search out the meanings of their own experience, and the therapist's role is to follow that process. In other words, the non-directive attitude is a belief in self-determination throughout the therapeutic process.

It is this belief in the right and capacity of the client to self-determine throughout the therapy process that made the Person-Centered approach revolutionary among mental health doctrines. This is why it needs to be considered a core conviction and attitude among Person-Centered therapists.

Why is this attitude so valuable? It helps protect the client from the therapist's errors of agenda, interpretation, and understanding.

An extreme and dramatic example of the therapeutic power of the non-directive attitude is the following description of a critical phase in my treatment of a client who was severely depressed as a result of an automobile accident that had disfigured her face. She was not ugly or scarred because the plastic surgery she underwent had been a success. Nevertheless, she experienced herself as losing her attractiveness as a woman. This, and feelings of depression, were the reasons she came to therapy. During the course of treatment, she discovered her husband was having an affair with her sister. She became increasingly suicidal. Her husband then decided to leave her, which increased her feelings of ugliness and worthlessness, resulting in further intense suicidal episodes. Then the husband, because of her "mental illness," decided to sue her for custody of their child. She lost the case in court. At this point her suicidal agony reached hospitalizing proportions.

Although hospitalizing the client was appealing for safety reasons, possible effects of stigmatization might further damage her precarious self-esteem. This raised the issue of short-term gain over long-term psychological change. After mutual exploration, we decided to maintain the client outside of the hospital.

Further disintegration and a "suicidal dance" between therapist and client ensued. This involved temporary drug use and periodic overdose/suicidal episodes. The client obtained drugs by deceiving physicians. I became skillful at reaching these physicians and stopping her drug flow. The drug use was a secondary, not primary, symptom. A confrontation and a battle to keep the client alive developed. Also, I became concerned about professional appropriateness and possible legal complications over not hospitalizing her (therapist agenda). My will about keeping the client alive and the possibility of hospitalization became increasingly forceful. I was fighting the client to keep the client alive.

A memorable challenge from the client occurred next. The client confronted me concerning the ultimate ontological right "to be or not to be." Why couldn't I accept her ultimate choice to live or die in the face of life's agony? Did I love her enough to let her end her suffering? Therapy had become an additional battle for her. I admitted I could not stand the pain of her death and that fighting for life was my value. I was clutching for the client's life out of my own and society's values. The client lacked the freedom "to be or not to be." She had to be valued enough to be granted this "terrible freedom."

At this point, the client had brought the non-directive attitude into focus in a highly challenging manner. This freedom and respect were at great risk. I was forced to listen to the client at a deep existential level. Again, the conflict was between short-term symptomatic gain and deeper, long-term personality change. I also had to be willing to relinquish control and assume responsibility. This is very different from the classical sociological understanding of a therapist's role. I decided to "be with" the client.

This was the turning point. Although I experienced fear and guilt over the risk taking, the client started to improve. She felt freedom and acceptance. She felt affirmed as a person with the capacity to choose. She felt trusted and she experienced the therapist as a person (vulnerability). We formed a deeper relationship. She was less isolated (anti-suicidal). The client later graduated from college, remarried, became employed and regained custody of her child. This is an example of psychological freedom: The client became self-empowered.

UNCONDITIONAL POSITIVE REGARD

Unconditional positive regard is a complex attitude, considered by Rogers (1957) as one of the "necessary and sufficient conditions" of psychotherapy. It is described as one of the core attitudes that needs to be natural for the therapist and should be brought to the therapeutic relationship.

Rogers describes UCPR as a warm acceptance of each aspect of the client's experience. There are no conditions of acceptance; it is non-judgmental. It means caring for the client.

In teaching UCPR, I present it as a multifaceted capacity that can be expressed in many different forms. Students are taught to identify those aspects of their personality that naturally express UCPR. They are taught to be natural with this attitude so as not to develop a role that a client will sense as artificial.

Unconditional positive regard can be expressed as love. There are times in therapy when the counselor can have feelings of love toward the client—not sexual love or a family love, but human loving of the client for his or her true self. One client expressed this as looking into the therapist's eyes and seeing herself expressed.

Rogers indicated that UCPR can be expressed as care. This can mean that what happens to the client really matters to the therapist on a personal level. I remember a client who was schizo-affective with secondary symptoms of drug abuse. She was also suicidal. One night a physician at the local hospital called to say that they were not sure they could save the client's life after a drug overdose. I remember crying for the client and the possible ending of her life. It really mattered. Her possible death was not an objective affair. I was quite relieved when word reached me that she had survived.

Compassion is another dimension of UCPR. This is the therapist's reaction to the client's suffering. Suffering receives little attention in professional writing about mental health. Suffering, however, is a major component in the seriously disturbed. I recall a dual-diagnosed, mentally retarded and schizophrenic client who was agonized, terrorized, and deeply pained over a hallucination involving an indistinct, purple, devilish apparition that laughed menacingly and mockingly at him. This would occur, very frequently, during each day while the client was trying to work in a rehabilitation center. One could not but experience compassion for this person who was going mad while trying to cope with the expectations of the agency.

Also, as Rogers indicated, non-judgmentalness is an aspect of UCPR. It can be illustrated as follows: The client, a paranoid-schizophrenic with suicidal and homicidal symptoms, was successfully treated without medications. After treatment, she expressed the conviction that treatment would have been impossible without my capacity to "separate the person from the disease." In this conviction, she is describing her experience of my non-judgmental attitude. The core necessity of UCPR is expressed.

In addition, according to Rogers, acceptance is a necessary component of UCPR. Perhaps acceptance can be modeled in this fashion. In teaching acceptance it is described as allowing the therapist to become pregnant with the meanings of the client. The client's meanings are welcomed deeply into your experience. You can accept the client's feelings inside. You can open yourself and experientially receive. The client is alive in you; the client experiences being taken in. This is difficult and critical when exploring suicidal, homicidal, and bizarre sexual feelings.

Nurturance is also considered part of UCPR. Nurturance is often expressed in therapy by a deeply sustaining and supportive attitude. For example, being available during a client's crisis is often significant. One client, who was suicidal, often called me when I was asleep. On these occasions she would hold a gun in her mouth, clicking it against her teeth in a way that I could hear it. The client experienced my response of "I'm here, I'm here" as supporting of her efforts not to impulsively shoot herself. A female therapist reported holding a male schizophrenic patient while he regressed into a fetal condition.

Valuing is communicating to clients aspects of their being that you, in fact, do value. Very often, in therapy, I will value a client's courage. A client was very hallucinatory, psychotic, and alcoholic. She came to therapy for many years and struggled with these problems. Even though she was psychotic and dangerous, she courageously struggled through to health. Very often, I expressed my admiration for her strength and responsibility.

Prizing is still another part of UCPR. It refers to an attitude of the therapist toward the life growth of the client. Many clients take small steps toward enhancing their existence. For example, a client who had been very psychotic improved sufficiently to enter a college computer-training program. I was clearly happy for this expansion of the client's life.

Last, but not least, is the attitude of respect. Respect conveys the feeling that clients have positive resources in themselves. You have the capacity to make this decision. A client who has been sexually abused, sodomized by his father and fixated with animal sexuality eventually, through treatment, humanized himself into a homosexual life-style. He then decided to leave treatment and enter the U.S. Marine Corps. The therapist was concerned that this could lead to a sexual episode with a psychotic relapse. However, the therapist respected the capacity of the client to make his own life decisions. The client did successfully complete service in the Marines. He came back stronger and more self-respecting.

THE EMPATHIC ATTITUDE

In a later phase of development, Rogers moved from concern with method to a more clearly defined phenomenological position (Zimring and Raskin, 1992). He states that the individual exists in a world of experience of which he or she is the center. He further states that the person reacts to the field as it is experienced. The perceptual field is reality for the client.

This emphasis on phenomenology leads to Rogers' emphasis on empathy (Rogers, 1957). He defines empathy as the therapist experiencing an accurate understanding of the client's experience. The therapist senses the client's world "as if" it were his own. More specifically, he indicates that the therapist is able to understand the client's feelings. The therapist is not in doubt about the client's feelings. His responses fit the client's mood, and his voice tone conveys the mood of the client.

In training mental health personnel to use their empathy, I outline the psychological structure of empathy so counselors can find empathy within themselves. First, empathy is conceived of as perceptual. The therapist can directly watch the face of the client to see the client's emotion. Second, empathy is emotional. The therapist can feel the client's emotion. This can be conceptualized as emotional resonance, similar to the resonance of tuning forks.

Third, empathy is communicative, meaning that the therapist can accurately verbalize the lived experience of the client.

Empathy with psychotics and retarded psychotics requires an *Einfuhlung*, a German word meaning "a feeling into" (Berger, 1987). The therapist probably does not know the psychotic experience, that is, dread over the loss of reality, feelings of unreality, hallucinatory and delusionary terror, deforming body experience, and so on. Because the therapist does not live the psychotic experience, he must assimilate it by gradually feeling into it. It requires an empathy for loss of self-sense and loss of reality—that is, ego loss.

What is it like to experience a psychotic hallucination? What is it like to experience walls shrinking? What is it like to experience time stopping? What is it like to experience your body undergoing sexual metamorphoses? Because of our sanity, these experiences are not easy to identify with. They are not easy to visualize, feel, or communicate. They are a range of experiences beyond our everyday psychological identification.

Einfuhlung (a feeling into) refers to a fuller grasp of the psychotic phenomenon. In grasping a hallucination, the first feeling into requires the therapist's sense of the *presence* of the hallucination for the client. This involves sensing the spatiality or temporality of the visual and auditory experience. This may involve following the client's gaze, body posture, bodily reactions, and so on. The second feeling into requires a literalization of the experience. The therapist needs to feel the client's *reality sense* of the apparition. He needs to know the perceived spatiality, movement, size, shape, color, lighting shades, and other perceptual details as if they were his own.

The therapist then needs to feel into the client's felt sense of the hallucination—how the client feels with the fear, distrust, humor, courage, ambivalence, or certainty about reality status. Finally, the therapist needs to know the *feeling status* of the hallucination, what feelings exist in it. The therapist must know the type of emotions that exist in this literal psychotic space.

To sum up, the therapist needs to grasp the client's *living with* the hallucination. He needs to know the hallucination as a "lived experience" (Makkreel, 1986). *Einfuhlung*, then, means to feel into a lived experience, to know it, to grasp the phenomenon.

GENUINENESS

Genuineness is another attitude the therapist should bring to the relationship. Rogers (1957) describes this as being congruent and integrated in therapy. It means, for Rogers, that the therapist is freely and deeply himself. It means that one is one's actual experience and that one is accurately represented in one's awareness.

Rogers further states that the counselor need not live a totally genuine existence. Rogers seems to restrict this attitude primarily to the therapy hour. I remember realizing I could expand genuineness to my personal sociometry. This would result in a self-selecting personal network. By being genuine, persons who accepted this mode would stay in the relationship and others would self-select out.

Genuineness must be related to the client. First, the client must be ready. If a client is anxiously concerned about homoerotic feeling and the therapist shares that experience or feeling, this can possibly be very threatening for the client. If the client were struggling for self-acceptance, a supportive genuineness could be helpful. Genuineness has to be relevant. The sharing of self has to be relevant to the client if it is to be meaningful. It is practically useless to share non-relevant experiences. If this is the case, then the counselor may be using the client for his own expressive needs. The self-sharing also needs to be real. The therapist must be careful that his sharing has not deteriorated into a role. The therapist may do the same sharing over and over again. If this happens, the counselor's existential presence acquires an artificial quality even if the events or feelings are real. The sharing becomes professionalized.

In teaching genuineness, I describe it as authenticity.[3] Being authentic is analyzed in three dimensions: (1) feeling your feelings; (2) expressing your feelings; (3) behaving your feelings. The student is also taught that utilizing these feelings is a matter of discrimination, responsibility, and choice.

Feeling one's feelings is important in therapy because it frees the therapist (Zucconi, 1984). It releases the visceral tension of blocked feelings and allows the therapist to feel more comfortable and relaxed. Because the therapist is less self-defensive, he is able to have greater presence for the client. This is particularly important when a client's psychotic feeling disturbs the therapist. Not infrequently, I have expressed my fear with violent clients. The congruence has helped the client with reality contact, engaging the more sensible part of the person.

Expressing the counselor's feelings is also an important aspect of therapy. Many deeply disturbed people have been subjected to conflicting, double-bound messages reflecting maximum incongruence (irreality). This has led to thought disorder and poor reality contact. However, too much congruence may frighten the psychotic client. Interpersonal intimacy often arouses extreme anxiety in the client. This is the difficult search and balance for the therapist of psychotic people. I recall working with a homicidal client who asked what I would do if she drew a gun to shoot. I replied I would defend myself. This greatly relieved the client because she felt she did not need to protect me. She further added she did not have to take responsibility for both sides of the relationship. It also helped her sense me as more real. At times, genuineness may be socially inappropriate, but therapeutically useful.

Behaving one's feelings is sometimes relevant. Often, I express genuine feelings of warmth and support by hugging, back-slapping, and so on. At other times I may express a helpful attitude by giving or lending money, if it helps the client's survival or life development.

Genuineness is also important as being the primary foundation for UCPR and empathy. These attitudes, if expressed in a congruent manner, become a more positive reality for the client. Genuineness of expression also functions as a model for the client to take more risks in personal self-expression. It illustrates the psychological safety and relationship potential in being oneself.

These three attitudes of unconditional regard, empathy, and congruence are the central tenets of a therapeutic relationship as presented by Rogers. They are considered fundamental to a "helping relationship" and are distinctly different from the classic neutral relationship of psychoanalysis and the objective attitude of behaviorism. They are a living sensitivity to the client's inner world. These three attitudes help to facilitate access to this inner world by both the therapist and the client. They represent the compassionate humanism of the therapist—the use of the therapist's human self. In the United States, this is why Rogers is considered the "Father of Humanistic Psychotherapy." More profoundly, they embody a way of being in a healing relationship.

LISTENING/REFLECTION

Because of Rogers' concern about directive and technical manipulativeness, he encouraged therapists' responses to be "listening/reflections." Listening can be described as essence and reflection as technique. Listening/reflection is consistent with Rogers' theory. In 1966, he concretized this consistency by describing listening/reflection as the vehicle for non-directiveness, empathy, and UCPR. Listening/reflection is non-directive because it follows the client's process. It is empathic because it expresses an understanding of the client's lived world. It conveys UCPR because it communicates deep acceptance through "taking the client in."

Reflective technique was first developed by Otto Rank (Rychlak, 1971). He used it as a cognitive method. The therapist reflected the content of what the client expressed. This enabled the therapist to more fully internalize the client's thinking. It also enabled the client to fully hear what he was saying. Rogers (1975), deeply influenced by Rank, creatively expanded reflection to include feeling.

Listening/reflection, even if not adopted within a Person-Centered approach to therapy, has value as a supplemental technique. Its general therapeutic value is one of relationship development. A client is more likely to form a relationship when he feels understood and is taken in empathetically. Being listened to does not arouse resistance as intensely (Stikkers, 1985) because of its phenomenological, ego-congruent nature.

The teaching of listening/reflection occurs in three phases. First, the student is asked to listen to a student client and then is asked to express what he heard to another training partner. This accentuates listening. Then, the student reflects the content of another trainee's expressions. This trains the student to hear the reality message clearly. Finally, the student reflects feeling. This aspect facilitates deeper self-exploration by the client.

Listening/reflecting with psychotic regressed clients sometimes requires a different emphasis. Very often, it is helpful to listen and reflect the content of the client's communication. This is important because content may be bizarre or irreal. Often the client is anxious about these communications because of the therapist's difficulty in understanding and empathy. It is reassuring for the client if the therapist reflects the content. Moreover, as Gendlin (1970) describes, affect is absent or "frozen" with these clients. Often, content is the only "entering." Content reflections may also give the client some psychological safety since they do not directly involve feeling. These clients are frequently afraid of experiencing or communicating their emotions.

Non-directiveness, UCPR, empathy, genuineness, and listening/reflection are the primary components of classical Rogerian therapy. A historical review of empirical studies is provided by Watson (1984).

NOTES

1. Raskin, N. *The Non-Directive Attitude*. Unpublished manuscript. (Also referred to in: Carl Rogers (1951), *Client Centered Therapy*, Boston: Houghton Mifflin, p. 29.)

2. Stubbs, Jeanne P. (1992). Individual Freeing in a Person-Centered Community Workshop. *The Person-Centered Journal*, Vol. 1 (1). Athens, Ga.: Iberian Publishing Co., pp. 38–49. Stubbs' concept of individual freeing is an example of liberation.

3. Lietaer, G. (1993). *Authenticity, Congruence and Transparency*. In D. Brazer (Ed.), *Beyond Carl Rogers*. London: Constable, pp. 17–46. The author describes transparency as the outer layer of therapist authenticity and congruence as the internal experience.

Chapter 2

Eugene Gendlin: An Interpretation

This chapter is a historically limited interpretation of Eugene Gendlin's "Person-Centered Phase" of the late 1950s, the 1960s and early 1970s. Gendlin's work during these years is the reason for his inclusion in the history of Person-Centered therapy. Later, Gendlin's writings are more experiential. Focusing and dreams (Gendlin, 1969, 1978, 1981, 1986) became his major concern.

HISTORY

During the 1940s and 1950s, Rogers defined his basic clinical method and relationship theory. During the 1960s he presented a new concept, Experiencing.

Rogers' 1961 article, titled "A Process Conception of Psycho-therapy," describes the stages of experiencing in therapy and explicitly acknowledges the influence of Gendlin's experiential theory. This formally introduced Experiencing into Person-Centered thought.[1] Hart (1970) describes the evolution of Person-Centered therapy into an experiential phase.

Philosophical Roots

Experiential thought is grounded in existential-pheno-menological philosophy (Gendlin, 1973). Fundamentally, experiential thinking is rooted directly in experience via Husserls' phenomenology. Second, experiential thought is anchored in Heidegger's existentialism, which conceives of man as "being in the world." Both views point toward man as being concretely in a life situation. Within that context, experiential thought is further influenced by Merleau-Ponty's philosophy of the "lived body," which is a description of concretely living in the organism. Additionally, experiential thought is affected by Buber's (1964) concern for the realm of the "inter-human." This philosophical notion results in an interactive conception of a human relationship.

THEORY

Gendlin (1964) defines his theory of Experiencing as concrete, bodily felt, and a process.

To define Experiencing as concrete means that a person can directly refer to it. She can directly attend to immediate experience and can perceive and relate it to her immediate phenomenology. In training students to identify Experiencing, I give them the following exercise:

Let yourself think about your day. Allow yourself to remember the early events of your morning. After these are clear, allow yourself to think of coming to the college. As you finish this, allow yourself to think of coming into this room. Finally, be aware of the immediacy of this room.

In this example, Experiencing is concrete and directly referred to by the student.

Experiencing has the quality of being bodily felt. It is sensed and experienced in the organism. It is a felt sense. In training students to identify the felt sense, I ask them to sense two or three significant concrete experiences. Students are then asked: How do these feel? How does experience A feel inside you? How does experience B feel inside you? Students are then asked to focus on the most intensely felt experience. Finally, students are asked to identify the attenuating feelings—sadness, anxiety, joy, and so on. This is the felt sense of the experience.

Finally, Experiencing is a process. It is a shifting from experience to experience, from experience A to experience B. Gendlin describes this as a felt shift. Again, students are asked to focus their concrete experiences and develop a felt sense. As the specific feelings emerge into the foreground, the students are asked to direct their awareness to the most intensely felt emotions. The students are next asked to stay with these feelings. This felt Experiencing then undergoes a visceral felt shift from felt experience A to felt experience B, and so on. These are process steps. A felt experience evolving to another felt experience is a process.

Experiencing is validated as an organismic process. Gendlin and Berlin (1961) found correlations between client reports of felt shift and galvanic skin responses. Don (1977) discovered correlations between phenomenologically reported felt shifts and electroencephalogram measurements.

Experiencing is formally defined as a concrete, bodily felt process. It is considered the essence of psychological change irrespective of clinical technique.

Gendlin (1979) divides the Experiencing process into four fundamental steps. The first step, as already described, is developing the experiential felt sense. The second step is differentiation. The third step is described as "carrying forward." The fourth step is interaction.

The experiential felt sense is a focused awareness coming from the body. It is not just feeling or emotion. It carries a felt sense of the organism's situation. It is a felt sense of "being in the world." It is a "listening" to one's self as one exists concretely. Initially, the felt sense may only yield an organismically correct right word. Gendlin describes this as a "handle" word. It is used as a reference point. We can return to handle words to resume our search for further elaboration of the felt sense.

This further elaboration of the felt sense is termed differentiation. Initially, as a person experiences a felt sense, it is complex and undifferentiated. With focused awareness, the felt sense becomes more perceivable or experiential. It elaborates itself from a vagueness to clearer and sharper detail. Experiential unit A becomes a+, a++, a+++, and so on.

As the felt sense becomes further explicated, it shifts, evolves, and moves forward in its felt meaning. This is called carrying forward. Carrying forward brings a bodily relaxation. The organism eases its tension; new thoughts and feelings emerge. This is the therapeutic change element. Carrying forward is when the situation is perceived differently. A shift in client meaning occurs.

After the organism has completed developing an experiential felt sense and has gone through the experiential process of differentiating and carrying forward, the organism becomes a "new meaning potential." It carries this new potential into Buber's "inter-human" and is both cause and effect of further interactive change. I, with my new meanings, affect you. You in turn further affect my new meanings. This process is interaction.

Experiencing, besides being a concrete, bodily felt process, is conceived of as a differentiating, carrying forward, interactive holistic activity of the organism.

REFLECTION/LISTENING: AN EXPERIENTIAL RESPONSE

Reflection, as indicated in Chapter 1, was introduced by Rank as a cognitive technique. Its function was to help the client hear her own thinking and to assist the therapist's understanding of a client's thought process.

Through Rogers, reflection later evolved into a feeling technique. The client felt understood, achieving greater emotional clarity and a sense of self. Rogers described reflection as conveying UCPR, empathy, and non-directiveness (see Chapter 1).

Gendlin (1968, 1974) conceptualizes reflection as an experiential response. Reflection facilitates the Experiencing process. Reflection now changes its theoretical function of conveying therapist attitudes (Rogers) to implementing a carrying forward of concrete, bodily felt process.

In training students to understand the meaning of reflection as an experiential response, I give them the following instructions: Reflect the content of the client's message. In Gendlin's language, I ask the student to grasp the client's sense of the situation which she is expressing. What is the client's *reality sense*? This often involves reflecting the concrete detail of how the client literally perceives reality. I am reminded of a client who would describe, for ten minutes straight, how each relative treated her: "My sister sees me this way, my brother sees me that way, my husband sees me 'so and so.' " She did not feel understood unless the therapist grasped the detail of her reality sense. If the therapist grasped her construction of the real, she felt relieved and then could move to her feelings. Very often, if clients have the reality content of their message understood, this releases them to express their feeling about the situation. *Reflection is always at the concrete.*

In the reflecting and experiencing process, a felt sense that is bodily felt will differentiate and carry forward into a "felt meaning." The undifferentiated, vague experience will evolve into a sharper, clearer, fine-tuned experience. The felt meaning is now more than body vagueness. It has evolved to include a cognitive, perceptual and intellectual grasp, by the client, of her situation. As Gendlin emphasizes, a felt meaning is always more than feeling or emotion; it includes an explicit cognitive grasp. A client, during a psychotherapy session, may say: "There's something there about my family. I don't know exactly what it is." The therapist may reflect: "There is some sense there about your family." The client may differentiate and carry forward, saying: "Yeah, it's something about how they make me feel no good." *Reflection is always at the felt aspect.*

Experiencing is a process. Experience A evolves into experience B. There is a felt shift, and the old experience carries forward to a new, more differentiated experience.

A client may angrily say: "I went to the store and bought five pounds of sugar for my mother."

The therapist may reflect the concrete and the felt aspect of the message: "You got some sugar for mom and it sounds like there was something angry in doing that."

The client may explicate further and say: "Yeah, I get angry at mom always pressuring me." This is a process shift. The feeling is clearer.

The therapist will then stay very close to the process and reflect: "The store is an example of your getting angry at mom's pressure." *Reflection is always at the process aspect.*

Reflection is always at the concrete felt process. Reflection is always at the Experiencing process.

Gendlin (1968) provides additional suggestions for therapist reflections that may further facilitate Experiencing. He suggests trying out directions for experiential moving forward. For example, a client may feel stuck. The therapist may say: "How does that stuckness feel?" Then the client may detail the "stuckness" and it becomes an experiential step in process. It then has the opportunity to become a felt sense, then change to differentiate and carry forward.

The next major point by Gendlin is very Person-Centered. He emphasizes that only the person knows her sense of the experiential "track" (process).

Gendlin concludes his clinical description by identifying what constitutes progress or improvement. Change, for Gendlin, is "referent movement" or "felt give." Referent movement means that the content moves from a vague felt sense to a clearer felt meaning—a movement in meaning from obscurity to clarity. A felt give refers to the organismic release or relaxation. It is the sense of "Aha! that feels true"; or, "That's it."

VARIATIONS IN EXPERIENTIAL PROCESS

Clinical exploration has revealed that different client populations have different modes of experiential process. Warner (1991) describes "fragile process," which seems to be characteristic of borderline, narcissistic, or schizoid personality disorders. Clients who have fragile process tend to experience core issues at either a high or low level of intensity.

Clients who experience high-intensity fragile process feel their experiences very strongly. Slight misunderstandings or slightly variant language are experienced as a significant break in empathy. Such breaks in empathy may be experienced as the therapist's attempt at the client's annihilation.

Clients who experience low-intensity fragile process have difficulty in experiencing their feelings. Their Experiencing is so subtle and lightly threaded that they can barely sense it. Low-intensity clients have difficulty in taking their feelings seriously. This often results in low-key, understated expression that often causes the listener to fail to grasp their significance. If this occurs, the client feels ignored or not valued.

Roy (1991) describes dissociated process in multiple personalities. Such persons often experience personality fragments on the margin of, or completely removed from, consciousness. These personality fragments often lack in experiential felt sense. As Roy indicates, such fragments may be expressed through halting and primitive symbolizations. I conceptualize such process as "pre-expressive" (Prouty, 1976). Pre-expressive process manifests itself in facial expression, body expression, situational expression, and word and utterance expression. Such expression is considered Pre-Experiential in that it is not directly phenomenological, but behavioral.

Sometimes, Roy used "body process" by reflecting the position of the client's lips. At other times, Roy would use "word process" by reflecting single words such as "face," "dark," "window," "cellar door," "hurt," "bleeding." As Roy (1991) states: "Dissociated material, whether it is as distinctive as separate personality, or much less so, must be experienced and allowed to live in the world." Roy describes a (facial) reflection: "You look angry." According to the client, this helped her make contact with the implicit angry feeling embodied in her face. This aided in making contact with her felt sense.

SUMMARY

Gendlin expands the explanation for therapeutic change from counselor attitudes to the client's Experiencing process. The phenomenology of Experiencing is described as concrete, bodily felt, and as a process. The phenomenology of the process steps are described as: felt sense, differentiating, carrying forward, and interaction. Reflection is always at the concrete, the felt sense, and the process. This theoretical reformulation of listening/reflecting as an experiential response is still consistent with non-directiveness (the client always best knows the experiential track). Differential patterns of process are described for different populations.

NOTE

1. Lietaer, G. (1983). On Client-Centered and Experiential Psychotherapy: An Interview With Eugene Gendlin. In Minsel, W. R. and W. Herff (eds.). *Research on Psychotherapeutic Approaches. Proceedings of the 1st European Conference on Psychotherapy Research, II.* Frankfurt am Main: Peter Lang, p. 81. Gendlin describes his greatest impact on Carl Rogers in terms of the process scale of psychotherapy.

Chapter 3

Rogers/Gendlin: Comparisons and Limitations

In the Person-Centered/Experiential movement, discussion takes place concerning the theoretical and clinical differences between Rogers and Gendlin. In part, this is because Rogers included Gendlin's influence in his writing. This inclusion is compounded by Gendlin's early writing on Person-Centered themes. However, the issues are currently relevant and require a more detailed examination.

COMPARISONS

Brodley (1990) compares Rogers and Gendlin on the issue of therapeutic trust in the client. She describes one difference in the following terms: In "client-centered therapy, the therapist functions consistently with trust in the client *as a whole person*; while in experiential therapy, trust is in the client's *experiencing process*."

She further states that a second difference lies in the Client-Centered trust in the attitudinal conditions as compared with the experiential therapist's trust in the experiential process. The attitudes are secondary. An extreme example of this can be found in Sasche (1990), who omits attitudinal conditions and defines the therapist's goal as an explication of Experiencing.

Concerning the issue of reflecting/listening, Brodley describes reflection as an "empathic following" that is characterized by the therapist's surrender of control or directivity. Listening is "more directed toward making the client feel and be aware of his Felt Sense. Listening is intended, by the therapist, to help the client refer to his Felt Sense." She identifies this subtle difference by referring to Hendricks' (1986) use of a "focused reflection" that emphasizes the felt sense instead of a surrendered following of process.

Brodley is saying that even though the literal, verbal form of the therapist's responses is essentially the same, the theoretical and communicative intent is different. The difference in intent, Brodley believes, affects the client. This raises questions at the level of concrete practice. Is the therapist primarily reliant on attitudinal or experiential facilitation of therapy?

Van Balen (1991) presents a very complicated discussion of the theoretical interface between the attitudes and Experiencing. First, he discusses Gendlin's criticism of Rogers that the client's conscious perception of the attitudes is the critical change point. Gendlin argues that the client "receives" the therapist's attitudes and that these enhance the interactive carrying forward of Experiencing. Second, Van Balen describes Experiencing, as it is used by Rogers, to be a function of the attitudes' loosening the defensive rigidity of the self-structure. Gendlin, in contrast, portrays change in self-experience as a function of the Experiencing process itself. Finally, Van Balen describes the role of Experiencing in each theorist. For Rogers, experiential change in therapy was *descriptive*. Evolving experiential stages were change manifestations. For Gendlin, Experiencing is *explanatory*. It is the psychological essence of therapeutic change.

My work (Prouty, 1992), consistent with other writers, considers Rogers and Gendlin as differentiated in terms of their major explanatory concepts. Rogers explains therapy primarily as a therapist construct—the attitudes. Gendlin explains therapy primarily as a client construct—the Experiencing process. In terms of therapy, Rogers seems to amplify the therapist side of the equation, while Gendlin seems to amplify the client side of the interaction. From a slightly different perspective than Van Balen's, I view Experiencing as articulated differently by the two theorists. For Rogers, Experiencing is a *result* of therapy. It is a dependent variable, a function of the attitudes. With Gendlin, Experiencing is a *cause* of therapy, an independent variable. It is the essence of therapeutic change. As described earlier, their use of the reflective/listening technique also differs. Rogers uses the technique to convey the attitudes of UCPR, empathy, and non-directiveness. Gendlin uses the technique to facilitate the Experiencing process.

In terms of formal theory construction, there are grounds for separating the two theories: differences in therapeutic cause, the locus of change, and the application of technique. Why, then, the historical impetus for their combination? I abundantly use each in actual practice because the attitudes express my therapeutic "being with." Experiencing expresses client process. Together, in my actual practice, they complement each other as non-directive Experiencing. They present a working paradigm. At the theoretical level, and even sometimes at the technical level, a polarization can occur. This polarization seems to be more a function of theoretical abstraction than the full reality of clinical practice. This interpretation, however, is limited to Gendlin's "Person-Centered phase."

LIMITATIONS

There are limitations to the use of Rogers' and Gendlin's theories and practice with severely regressed, low-functioning clients. These are most evident with retarded and schizophrenic populations. The issue starts with Rogers' conviction that Client-Centered therapy is not appropriate for mentally retarded clients. Very early, Rogers (1942) expressed the view that retarded clients lack the autonomy and introspective skills required for Client-Centered therapy. Ruedrich and Menolascino (1984) believe this has a considerable limiting effect on psychotherapy for the mentally retarded, producing a paucity of efforts. It is only in recent years that Peters of the Netherlands (1981, 1986a, 1992), Badelt of Germany (1990), and Portner of Switzerland (1990) have produced practice papers applying "classical" Client-Centered therapy with the retarded.

Further limitations involving schizophrenic clients are reported from the Wisconsin Project (Rogers et al., 1967). In terms of the major constructs of relationship and Experiencing,[1] they empirically found that regardless of the therapist's attitudes, patients perceived low levels of these core attitudes, and there was no significant movement in the Experiencing process during therapy for the schizophrenic clients. They also found there was no significant difference in the Experiencing process between the treatment group and the control group.

I suggest that theoretical limits of Rogers might also have impeded the Wisconsin work (Prouty, 1990). Many schizophrenic clients are psychologically isolated and withdrawn, that is, out of contact with the therapist. Rogers' "first condition" of a therapeutic relationship is "psychological contact. Unfortunately, Rogers provides no theoretical definition of psychological contact. Additionally, he does not provide any technique for restoring psychological contact if it is impaired. Last, he proceeds theoretically as if contact between therapist and client were assumed. In essence, Rogers does not provide any theoretical or clinical guidance for psychological contact, often a major problem for these clients.

In addition, there are definitional problems in Gendlin's conception of schizophrenia (Prouty, 1990). Gendlin (1970) states:

My conception of the illness: It is not so much what is there, as what is not here. The interactive Experiential process is lacking, stuck, deadened in old hurt stoppages and in the disconnection from the world. The psychosis is the curtailment or cessation of the interaction process of feeling and events.

This describes the absence or impairment of Experiencing in the schizophrenic population. It means that the element of therapeutic change (Experiencing) is not available for treatment. This leaves the somewhat paradoxical situation of defining schizophrenia by a theoretical construct that is impaired or absent. This, of course, is a non-process definition.

Further definitional problems are presented by Gendlin's description of hallucinations as "structure bound" (Gendlin, 1964). Structures are perceived, by the client, "as such." Second, the client experiences hallucinations as "not his." Third, structure-bound experience is isolated. It is not working in the felt functioning of the organism. Fourth, the felt functioning is rigid (not in process). "Structure bound" is characterized as static, repetitious, and unmodifiable experience. This also is a non-process description.

Again, this presents a problem. I describe it elsewhere in the following way:

Experiential Process is the essence of therapeutic change; yet, it is the element that is impaired or absent. Gendlin's phenomenological description of the hallucinatory Structure Bound "State" yields the problematic of how to turn a *Non-Process* Structure into a *Process* Structure. (Peters, 1992).

Rogers' hesitancy with retarded clients, combined with the empirical findings of the Wisconsin schizophrenic project and his theoretical limitations concerning contact, set the stage for a necessary revision of Person-Centered thinking and practice with these populations.

Gendlin's phenomenological descriptions of "experiential absence" or "experiential impairment" as characteristic of schizophrenic clients also set the stage for a fundamental question. Theoretically and clinically, how do we move from a non-process to a process conception? This also sets the stage for revising and evolving experiential thought.

What type of theorizing and practice can carry us over these boundaries?

NOTE

1. On a positive note, where experiential process did occur, it was related to the attitudes. Clients receiving the highest levels of therapeutic attitudes evidenced reduction in schizophrenic pathology. Treated clients showed better hospital discharge rates and improved Thematic Apperception Test (TAT) protocols. See Rogers et al. (1967). The Findings in Brief. In C. Rogers (ed.), *The Therapeutic Relationship and Its Impact: A Study of Psychotherapy with Schizophrenics*. Madison, Wis.: University of Wisconsin Press, 1967, 80–81, 85.

Part II

EVOLUTIONS IN PERSON-CENTERED THEORY

Chapter 4

Pre-Therapy: An Essay in Philosophical Psychology

THE CONCRETE PHENOMENON "AS ITSELF"

Pre-Therapy, consistent with Person-Centered, Gestalt, and Experiential psychotherapies, rests within the existential phenomenological tradition. It is a "pointing at the concrete" (Buber, 1964). Its method is based on a conception of the concrete phenomenon "as itself."

The concrete phenomenon as itself can be clarified in terms of first, the "concrete attitude" of the client, and second, the concreteness of the phenomenon as "naturalistic," "self-indicative," and "desymbolized."

The Concrete Attitude

Gurswitch (1966) describes a phenomenological study of brain-damaged patients by Gelb and Goldstein, who found that these patients had a "concrete attitude," as distinguished from a "categorical attitude." A patient with a concrete attitude experiences many shades of the same color as different colors. A person with a categorical attitude who is not brain-damaged would describe the many shades as the same color.

The brain-damaged person cannot categorize; meanings are perception-bound and not abstracted essences. Arieti (1955), also influenced by Goldstein, found the same concrete attitude among schizophrenics.

Pre-Therapy, because it primarily focuses on mentally retarded and schizophrenic clients, is especially sensitive to developing a conception of the phenomenon consistent with the concrete attitude of these populations and the extraordinarily concrete responses of Pre-Therapy.

The "As Itself"

The "as itself" is naturalistic. Farber (1959, 1967), and Riepe (1973) propose a phenomenology that describes phenomena as they appear "naturally" in consciousness.

This is done *without* the suspension of the natural attitude toward experience, or a phenomenological reduction to an essence (Jennings, 1992).[1] The concrete phenomenon is described as it manifests itself "as itself."

The "as itself" is self-indicative. The concrete phenomenon is "Absolutely Self-Indicative" (Sartre, 1956). This means the phenomenon is "what it is, absolutely, for it reveals itself as it is. The phenomenon can be described, as such, for it is absolutely indicative of itself." Again, the phenomenon is described "as itself."

The "as itself" is desymbolized. The concrete phenomenon is described as "desymbolized" (Scheler, 1953). Scheler states:

Something can be Self-Given only if it is no longer given merely through any sort of symbol; in other words, only if it is not meant as the mere fulfillment of a sign that is previously defined in some way or other. In this sense, phenomenological philosophy is a continual de-symbolization of the world.

In other words, the phenomenon appears non-symbolically "as itself."

The "as itself": An example. The "as itself" is a primordial, perceptual consciousness of the phenomenon. This example is drawn from a non-verbal memory I had as an infant.

The awareness of the world is of lying on my back in a crib. On my right side, at an even height with my body and at about a 15 degree angle, is a window. Through the window, at a medium distance, there is a tree. The tree is black and gray without leaves. The limbs reach toward the sky like bony fingers. The sky is gray-black, like dusk.

My awareness of self was two-fold. First, the experience "belonged" to consciousness. Consciousness was sensed as the locus of experience. Second, consciousness was aware of itself as consciousness "of." Consciousness grasped itself through the act of intentionality.

The awareness of "other" was the unrecognized figure of my mother entering the scene. The experience was of her arms picking me up and the correlated swirl of bright light. The sensation was of being wrapped in a blanket and carried on her shoulder and being rocked very slowly. The sense of "other" was present and separate.

This primordial consciousness of world, self, and other is foundational for the development of an existential consciousness.

EXISTENTIAL CONSCIOUSNESS

Existential consciousness is characterized by: the existential structures of consciousness, existential contact, and existential autism.

The Existential Structures of Consciousness

Pre-reflective consciousness is described as the immediately sensed perception of lived experience, or *Erleben*, in German.

In the language of Merleau-Ponty, the world, self, or other can be described as "Concrete A-Priori" (Merleau-Ponty, 1962; Mallin, 1979). World, self, and other are the natural and categorical "revelatory absolutes" of immediate consciousness through which particular concrete existents manifest themselves.

The existential structures of consciousness are characterized by a pre-reflective consciousness (lived experience) of the world, self, or other (existence) as concrete phenomenon (naturalistic, self-indicative, desymbolized).

Existential Contact

This contact of pre-reflective consciousness with the concrete phenomenon of the world, self, and other is described as "existential contact."

Husserl (Speigelberg, 1978) conceived all consciousness as "intentional"; that is, all consciousness is consciousness *of* something. All consciousness "intends" an "object." Existential contact is the natural, alternating movement of immediate pre-reflective consciousness toward the natural presence of the world, self, or other. Consciousness naturally and alternately moves toward existence.

Existential Autism

Impairment of existential contact due to psychological or organic disorder results in existential autism (Laing, 1990; Dosen, 1983). The rich, meaningful, everyday, natural, pre-reflective consciousness is no longer "intentional" (toward, with, or about). Consciousness is no longer contactful.

Existence becomes a "void of significance," a failure in coherence. Consciousness becomes empty, an isolated shell of meaninglessness. Consciousness is not related to existence. It lives without the "creation of meaning" that comes from primordial contact with the natural absolutes of the world, self, or other.

Pre-Therapy, in existential-phenomenological terms, is the movement of consciousness from existential autism to existential contact.

NOTE

1. Jennings, J. L. (1992). The Forgotten Distinction between Psychology and Phenomenology. In Miller, R. (ed.), *The Restoration of Dialogue: Readings in the Philosophy of Clinical Psychology*. Washington, D.C.: American Psychological Association, pp. 293–305. This section contains a detailed discussion of Husserl's views on naturalism and "bracketing."

Chapter 5

Pre-Therapy as a Theoretical System

THE MEANING OF "PRE"

To understand Pre-Therapy, it is useful to examine the prefix "pre." "Pre," in the context used here, refers to pre-conditions. Several analogies convey this functional and logical meaning.

In the field of art, painters generally use an instrument to function, such as a brush. A modern artist may use a manufactured wooden handle with bristles. A caveman might have used a wooden tree branch with leaves or moss. In either case, a brush is typically a necessary pre-condition of painting. The modern painter often uses oil paints. The artist from prehistoric times may have used berry juices or animal fats. In either situation, the function of painting requires a fluid medium as a pre-condition. Finally, the prehistoric artist would require a surface. He or she may have used a cave wall. The modern artist may purchase a manufactured canvas. Functionally, both require a relatively flat surface. This is another necessary pre-condition of painting.

Another analogy can be drawn from the field of reading development. In order to read, children must possess the psychological capacity known as symbol recognition. Second, they must have the neuromuscular capacity to move their eyes from left to right. Third, they must have the memory capacity to retain information. Symbol recognition, neuromuscular capacity, and memory function as the pre-conditions of reading.

Each of these analogies presents the meaning of "pre" as the logically necessary conditions of their particular functions (painting or reading). What I have described are the *necessary* conditions of painting and reading.

Transposing this analysis to Rogers' work in clinical psychology one might ask: What are the *necessary conditions* of a therapeutic relationship? This, of course, *deconstructs* Rogers' conception of the "necessary and sufficient conditions." It enables us to ask: What is *necessary*? What is *sufficient*? This further enables us to ask: What are the necessary *pre-conditions* of a therapeutic relationship?

Many clients are not fully capable of maintaining therapeutic relationships, as is the case with the schizophrenic and retarded/psychotic populations. What are the necessary conditions to form a relationship? This deconstruction of Rogers' definition into necessary and sufficient components allows us to examine it in a new context. It allows us to think in terms of pre-relationship. What goes on before we can form a classical Client-Centered relationship? The first meaning of "pre" is pre-relationship.

In a similar manner, we can examine the concept of Experiencing. As many of the schizophrenic and retarded/psychotic clients have no easy access to a therapeutic relationship; they cannot easily access their Experiencing. This is probably due to a lack of "internal contact" resulting from a strong autistic component (Minkowski, 1970; Dosen, 1983). As explained in Chapter 3, schizophrenic clients do not seem able to process their Experiencing. When this is the case, we face a problem similar to that which occurs with a therapeutic relationship. What is the necessary condition of Experiencing? What has to be psychologically operative before Experiencing can occur? This new train of thought leads us to the language pre-experiential.

When we think clinically about pre-relationship and pre-Experiential, we are exploring how to help clients who are *relationship or experientially impaired and cannot use these functions for therapy*. This is the genesis of Pre-Therapy; it describes the clinical search for a mode of treatment for those who cannot fully use relationship or Experiencing processes.

The logic of the pre-conditions of relationship and Experiencing evolves into a wider theoretical question. What are the pre-conditions, the necessary conditions of psychotherapy in general? What are the psychological functions necessary for psychotherapy? The deconstructed theory of Rogers' necessary and sufficient conditions gives us direction. Psychological contact is the necessary condition of psychotherapy. This is the foundation for an evolved Pre-Therapy.

PSYCHOLOGICAL CONTACT

Pre-Therapy is a theory of psychological contact. It is rooted in Rogers' conception of psychological contact as the first condition of a therapeutic relationship. It is also rooted in Perls' (1969) conception of ego as a "contact function." Pre-Therapy is the development or restoration of the functions necessary for a therapeutic relationship and Experiencing. Pre-Therapy, described in general terms, develops the *necessary psychological capacities for psychotherapy*. It assists those clients who are impaired in the psychological functions required for treatment to occur.

Psychological contact, as a theoretical system, is described as: contact reflections, contact functions, and contact behaviors (Peters, 1986b); Leijssen and Roelens, 1988).

Contact reflections refer to counselor technique. They represent evolution in the Person-Centered/Experiential method (see Chapters 1 and 2). Reflection for Rogers embodied the attitude; reflection for Gendlin facilitates the Experiencing process. Reflection for Pre-Therapy develops psychological contact.

Contact functions refer to the internal psychological functions of the client. They are an evolution in Perls' concept of psychological contact as an ego function.[1] They are described as reality contact, affective contact, and communicative contact.

Contact behaviors refer to specific behaviors to be measured so as to illustrate the outcome of Pre-Therapy. Reality, affective and communicative contact are the emergent behaviors that represent changes in contact.

Contact Reflections

Contact reflections have the theoretical function of developing psychological contact between therapist and client when the client is incapable of reality, affective, or communicative contact. They are applied when there is not sufficient contact to implement psychotherapy.

Contact reflections are concrete in that they are extraordinarily literal and duplicative. They are empathic to the specific concrete particularity of the client's regressed efforts at expression and communication. This is the core empathy.

There are five contact reflections (Karon and Vanderbos, 1981): situational reflections (SR), facial reflections (FR), word-for-word reflections (WWR), body reflections (BR), and reiterative reflections (RR).

Situational contact refers to reflections at the client's situation, environment, or milieu. For example, a therapist may situationally reflect:"Tom is playing with the red ball." Another situational reflection may be: "You are holding the chair." These types of reflections help make reality contact. They facilitate existential contact with the *world*.

Facial contact describes reflections of facial affect. Many psychotic and retarded clients, due to psychosocial isolation, over-medication, and institutionalization, do not experience themselves as the locus of emotion or feeling. They often exist in a state of emotional autism, numbness, or absence. Often, the feeling exists in a pre-expressive form in the face. Arthur Burton (1973) suggests that the face has the phylogenetic function of emotional expressivity. It has evolved through mammalian biological development for that purpose.

Facial reflections may be demonstrated by the following: "You look sad," or "You look scared." Another example might be: "Your face looks happy." The therapist is "inter-humanizing" the emotion or feeling with the client. Facial contact or reflections have the theoretical function of developing affective contact or existential contact with the *self*.

Word-for-word contact or reflections mean the literal "welcoming" repetition of singular words, multiple word fragments, or fragments of meaning that the client expresses. Many schizophrenic clients, due to their use of neologisms, word-salads, and echolalia, are often incoherent. The same difficulties occur with the retarded/psychotic, only these difficulties are compounded communicatively by mental retardation. In either case, the client's speech seems to flow coherently, then incoherently, coherently, incoherently, and so on. For example, the client may say: "[incoherent word, incoherent word], house, [incoherent word, incoherent word], tree." The therapist would selectively reflect "house," then "tree." This word-for-word reflection reinforces the client sense of self as a communicator. This is perhaps a poetic empathy as reflected in Buber's "Response" of "I" to "Thou." Word-for-word reflections develop communicative contact or existential contact with the *other*.

Body contact refers to reflections of the client's body. Schizophrenic and retarded/psychotic clients manifest echopraxia, catatonia, and bizarre body posturing. The significance of the body in the psychotherapy of schizophrenia was researched by Mauerer-Groeli (1976). From the psychoanalytic perspective, that author found improved ego functions as a result of body therapy with a large number of psychotic clients.

In Pre-Therapy, there are two kinds of body reflections. The first is an empathic body duplication by the therapist. This is illustrated by Prouty and Cronwall (1990). Cronwall describes a depressed and profoundly retarded client whose major behavior in therapy was to "make-believe" he was turning the steering wheel of a car. There was no language or contact with the therapist. The client only drove his imaginary steering wheel. The therapist's body reflected this by turning her own steering wheel and duplicating the body movements of the client.

The second body reflection in Pre-Therapy is verbal. For example, a therapist may reflect catatonic posturing: "Your arm is in the air. Your body is very rigid." These kinds of body or verbal reflections help assist the client experience his body as a "me" or self-experience. This can be the resolution of a very primitive trauma or lack of development.

Re-contact or reiterative reflections refer not to a specific technique, but to a principle. The principle is: If a specific reflection succeeds in making psychological contact, repeat it. Repeating the psychological contact maximizes the opportunity to develop a relationship or to facilitate Experiencing.

There are two types of re-contact: immediate and longer term. An example of immediate re-contact is drawn from Prouty and Cronwall (1990). A profoundly retarded client, who had no contact with the therapist, utters a word: "Candy." The therapist immediately re-contacts or reiterates "Candy." The client then responds, more intentionally, louder, "Candy." The client then gradually says, "Napkin," "Plates," "Party." By reiterating "Candy," the client's communication expanded. Van Werde (1990) describes a therapeutic sequence with a psychotic, mentally retarded girl who was diagnosed as schizo-affective. The therapist performed a longer-term, reiterative re-contact. The therapist, earlier in the session, had body reflected: "You touched your forehead." Some minutes later, the therapist made a reiterative reflection: "You touched your forehead." The client then proceeded to say, "Grandma." This interchange evolved into the client expressing genuine and congruent feeling about her grandmother.

Pre-Therapy, by using contact reflection, tends to reduce psychotic expression and facilitate more realistic communication embodying the world, self, or other (reality, affective, and communicative contact).

Contact Functions

The contact functions, in psychological terms, represent an expansion of Perls' concept of "contact as an ego function." They are conceived as awareness functions and described as reality, affective, and communicative contact.

The development or restoration of the contact functions is the necessary pre-condition for psychotherapy. They function as the theoretical goals of a Pre-Therapy.

Reality contact. Reality contact (world) is defined as the awareness of people, places, things, and events. If we describe the world as we concretely experience it, we see that we live with things. Our world is an infinite thematic field of things. Things are part of our living existence. We turn handles, we throw balls, we smell flowers, we touch stones, we use toasters, we see by electric light bulbs. Things are a definite part of our reality sense.

Even if we do not have intimate relationships, our world is peopled. Everywhere, there are people. We live with people. People are on the bus, in the airplane, at the physician's office, on the island of Tahiti, and so on. Again, there is an infinite thematic of people. Even if we live alone on an island, there are people in our heads. We would talk to them. People are a concrete part of our reality sense.

Mankind is spatially constructed. We live "in" space. Spatiality is a concrete part of our reality. Things and people are bound up with space. The ball is here. The ball is there. I am here. You are there. These are the meanings of place. Place is a deep part of our reality sense. Spatiality is also an infinite thematic.

Mankind is also temporally constructed. We live "in" time. Time is also a concrete part of our reality. Things, people, and places have their occurrence in time. This is the concrete meaning of event. I am here now. You are there now. We were there then. We will be married in November. Time is an infinite thematic.

People, places, things, and events are the concrete, yet infinite thematics of our "being-in-the-world."

Affective contact. Affective contact (self) is our response to the world or other. Affective contact is defined as awareness of moods, feelings, and emotions. Moods, feelings, and emotions are different phenomenological and concrete forms of affect.

Mood is affect that is subtle, diffuse, and general. Often, a mood is background sensing. It is a coloring of events. I can go to a football game and experience an anxious or depressed mood that feels separate from the current reality. The mood also has a low intensity to it. It often lacks direct focus.

Feeling is more pronounced affect. A feeling is clearer and it has a specific locus. It is in response to the event itself. I feel this or that about this or that. The intensity of feeling is stronger than that of a mood. It is not as subtle; it is more articulated as an affective experience. Instead of being background, it is more foreground about the event. I feel sad that my grandmother is deceased and is no longer here to care about me.

Emotion is affect that is considerably more intense and more clearly linked to an event. It is sharp, clear, and more detailed. Emotion has the psychological quality of being totally foreground. My emotional reaction is rage if you are attacking my child or my wife.

Moods, feelings, and emotions are an infinite thematic of our contact with existence.

Communicative contact. Communicative contact is defined as the symbolization of reality (world) and affect (self) to others.

Communicative contact is more than the transmission of information. It is the meaningful expression of our perceived world and self to others. It conveys denotative and connotative meanings from our experiential universe. It reveals to the other. It enables psychological contact with the other.

Communicative contact primarily refers to social language. We concretely live in language. It is an infinite thematic of our being-in-the-world. We think in language. We speak in language. We create in language. We even die in language, as on tombstones. One merely has to experience living in a culture with a different language to experience the psychological significance of language.

The Contact Functions in Therapy

A therapeutic vignette illustrates contact reflections resulting in the restoration of the contact functions in a chronic schizophrenic woman. It also illustrates the restoration of psychological contact as a pre-condition of relationship.

Dorothy is an old woman who is one of the more regressed women on X ward. She was mumbling something [as she usually did]. This time I could hear certain words in her confusion. I reflected only the words I could clearly understand. After about ten minutes, I could hear a complete sentence. (For a therapist reflection key, see page 38.)

Client:	Come with me.
Therapist: WWR	Come with me.
	[The patient led me to the corner of the day room. We stood there silently for what seemed to be a very long time. Since I couldn't communicate with her, I watched her body movements and closely reflected these.]
Client:	[The patient put her hand on the wall.] Cold.
Therapist: WW-BR	[I put my hand on the wall and repeated the word.] Cold.

	[She had been holding my hand all along, but when I reflected her, she would tighten her grip. Dorothy began to mumble word fragments. I was careful to reflect only the words I could understand. What she was saying began to make sense.]
Client:	I don't know what this is anymore. [Touching the wall: reality contact.] The walls and chairs don't mean anything anymore. [Existential autism.]
Therapist: WW-BR	[Touching the wall.] You don't know what this is anymore. The chairs and walls don't mean anything to you anymore.
Client:	[The patient began to cry: affective contact. After a while she began to talk again. This time she spoke clearly: communicative contact.] I don't like it here. I'm so tired . . . so tired.
Therapist: WWR	[As I gently touched her arm, this time it was I who tightened my grip on her hand. I reflected.] You're tired, so tired.
Client:	[The patient smiled and told me to sit in a chair directly in front of her and began to braid my hair.]

This vignette begins to express Pre-Therapy as a therapeutic theory and philosophy. It illustrates the use of contact reflections to facilitate the contact functions (reality, affect, communication).

In existential/phenomenological terms, this vignette illustrates a resolution of existential autism (loss of contact with the world, self, and other) and the development of existential contact (contact with the world, self, and other. Clearly, the existential structures of consciousness are reintegrated with existence. This case also illustrates another dimension of Pre-Therapy. It shows the movement from a pre-expressive mode of communication to an expressive mode of communication.

Contact Behaviors

Contact behaviors are the emergent behavioral changes that result from the facilitation of the contact functions through the use of contact reflections. They are the operationalized aspect of psychological contact.

Reality contact (world) is operationalized as the client's verbalization of people, places, things, and events.

Affective contact (self) is operationalized as the body or facial expression of affect. For example, a bodily expression of affect may be: "John angrily kicks the chair." A facial expression of affect may be: "John looks sad." Affective contact may also be operationalized through the use of feeling words. The client may use affective language such as "sad," "angry," "happy," and so on.

Communicative contact (other) is operationalized as the client's verbalization of social words or sentences.

What is being measured is the expression of reality, affect, and communication. On a clinical level, the measurement reflects the shift in a client from a pre-expressive to an expressive level. In addition, we are measuring the client's increased expression about the world, self, or other.

Pilot studies. The measurement process is as follows. A Pre-Therapy scale is constructed for three dimensions: reality, affect, and communication. Dimension I (reality) is scorings for people, places, things, and events. Dimension II (affect) is scorings for facial expression, bodily expression, and feeling words. Dimension III (communication) is scorings for words and sentences. These three scoring dimensions measure movement from a pre-expressive to an expressive communication about the world, self, or other.

The procedural steps are: (1) Clients are tape-recorded through all sessions; (2) the recordings are transcribed to scoring sheets; and (3) raters are trained for scoring competency.

Pilot studies (Prouty, 1985), using single-case observations, present data supporting the construct validity (Christensen, 1991) of psychological contact.

Table 1 describes nine pairs of mean scores, from two independent raters, over a three-month period with a retarded schizophrenic client. Mean scores per month are compared between raters. These scores have a correlation coefficient of 0.9966, with a p-value of 0.0001, presenting strong evidence against the null hypothesis of no correlation. The pairwise t-test resulted in a value of 0.9864 with a p-value of 0.3528. These results indicate no difference between rater scorings.

Table 2 describes 24 pairs of scorings from two independent raters through a single session of Pre-Therapy with a schizo-affec-

Table 1
RAC Mean Frequency per Standardized Sessions

Three-Month Intervals February–October Rater 1, 2		
February—April		
	Rater 1	**Rater 2**
Reality	59	48
Affect	27	27
Communication	71	77
May—July		
Reality	149	175
Affect	11.5	11.5
Communication	110	100
August—October		
Reality	379	446
Affect	17	13
Communication	214	225
Correlation Coefficient 0.9966	p-value	0.0001
t-value 0.9864	p-value	0.3528

tive, retarded client. Scores are drawn from percentiles 1–20, 40–60, and 80–100. In other words, the beginning, middle, and end of the session were evaluated. A correlation coefficient of 0.9847 with a p-value of 0.0001 was obtained. The pairwise t-test produced a value of 2.3738 with a p-value of 0.0526. These results indicate no difference between scorings at 1 percent or 5 percent levels of significance.

An independent pilot study (De Vre, 1992) further confirmed construct validity and also developed evidence for reliability. De Vre and her colleagues, Van Werde and Deleu, utilizing the Pre-Therapy scale, measured three data samples from three clients. Two clients were described as chronic schizophrenics, and the third

Table 2
RAC Frequencies—Single Session

	Reality				Affect			Communication	
	pe	pl	ev	th	f	b		w	s
R-1	9	3	4	6 (22)	3	1 (4)		3	6 (9)
R-2	10	5	2	7 (24)	2	1 (3)		4	8 (12)
R-1	43	16	31	15 (105)	5	7 (12)		40	17 (57)
R-2	42	14	28	12 (96)	5	8 (13)		36	17 (53)
R-1	34	6	17	4 (61)	0	8 (8)		19	16 (35)
R-2	29	5	13	4 (51)	0	8 (8)		11	14 (25)

Correlation coefficient　　0.9847　　　　　p-value　0.0001

t-value 2.3738　　　　　　　　　　　　p-value　0.0526

1% or 5% Level of significance

was diagnosed as a borderline psychotic. All three clients were measured under hospitalized conditions.

The first measure of agreement (Cohen, 1968) between two raters was kappa 0.39. With refinement of the English to Flemish translation, the second measure, with the same raters and a second client, was kappa 0.76. A third measure, with the same raters and a third client, was kappa 0.87. These measures of agreement were statistically significant at 0.00005.

A reliability measure was developed by having two independent psychiatric nurses instructed in the use of the Pre-Therapy scale. The rating of the first data sample was 0.39. The nurses' level of agreement was kappa 0.7 at a 0.0005 level of significance.

These U.S. and Belgian pilot studies provide some indication for the valid and reliable measurability of contact behaviors.

NOTE

1. Perls, F. S., R. Hefferline, and P. Goodman. (1951). *Gestalt Therapy: Excitement and Growth.* New York: Julian Press, p. 229. In a structural sense, Perls sees the dynamic units constituting the system self as a form of contact (p. 224). Perls then goes on to say that reality is given in

moments of good contact—a unity of awareness, motor response and feeling (p. 372). Perls further describes a definition of perceptual contact as a sequence of figures forming against grounds (p. 403); Perls, F. S. (1976). *The Gestalt Approach and Eyewitness to Therapy*. New York: Bantam Edition, p. 17. Perls describes a functional relationship between a human being and his environment in terms of a contact boundary. It is at the contact boundary that psychological events take place. Perls further states that our thoughts, acts and emotions are our way of experiencing and meeting these boundary events (p. 17); Polster, E., and M. Polster. (1974). *Gestalt Therapy Integrated*. New York: Vintage Books, p. 103. According to the Polsters, the contact boundary is the point at which one experiences the "me" in relation to the "not me." Through contact, both are more clearly experienced (p. 103).

Chapter 6

The Practice of Pre-Therapy

Thus far, I have described Pre-Therapy in terms of philosophical psychology and as a theoretical system. This chapter will focus on clinical practice, presenting materials from the treatment of schizophrenics and mentally retarded/dual-diagnosed clients.

PRACTICE OBSERVATIONS

Pietrzak notes that for Pre-Therapy, the "techniques are simple, but the practice is difficult."[1] These practice observations are added to the techniques to enhance their usage.

Since Rogers emphasizes empathy as one of the core conditions, Pre-Therapy emphasizes "empathic contact." However, this empathic contact has a different focus than the client's frame of reference. The focus of empathy is the client's regressed, incoherent efforts at pre-expressive communication. *The therapist does not know the client's frame of reference*. The empathy is for the client's effort at developing coherent experience and expression, perhaps a form of concretizing the self-formative tendency during these primitive phases of therapy.

A second level of empathy concerns the concreteness of pre-expressive behavior. The contact reflections need to be extraordinarily concrete. They are not focused on the generalized "essence" of meaning, but on the literal expressive behavior. *The empathy is for the concrete particularity of behavioral expression.*

A third level of empathy concerns the increase of psychotic expression as a function of Pre-Therapy. The client needs to get worse before she can get better. The therapist needs to be empathic to an increase in delusional and hallucinatory expression, as well as to an increase in bizarre communication (strange body postures, language disturbances, etc.). This means being empathic to the lived experience of the psychosis itself. This is, of course, the opposite of behavioral or chemical management.

Other empathic concerns involve temporality and spatiality (Binswanger, 1958). Often, experiences of time and space are altered. One client reports being terrified of time stopping. Another client reports being horrified by her experience of a room shrinking. The phenomenology of time is slowed during depression and accelerated for manic episodes. The spatial phenomenology is often altered in hallucinatory states because the hallucination occupies a literal space (Havens, 1962).

Empathy for temporal and spatial experience is very important in approaching chronic regressed clients. Very often they are frightened of contact. Spatiality becomes a sensitive dimension. One forward step too close can be overwhelming and disrupt relationship formation.

The tempo of contact is also a sensitive dimension. Rapidly given reflections may overwhelm the client. Multiple reflections, given at one time, can also alienate the client. Conversely, too few reflections, expressed too slowly, may cause the loss of contact. It is important to understand that the therapist is entering a phenomenological "world" and that one needs to be empathic to the experiential structures of that world.

CLIENTS

The first case history concerns a young, catatonic, schizophrenic male who had been treated with electro-shocks, as well as multiple chemical interventions. The treatment vignette is drawn from a

12-hour period during which the therapist was able to restore verbal communication.

The second case history involves a mentally retarded, schizophrenic young woman. The description is about the resolution of a psychotic episode and presents Pre-Therapy as a form of crisis intervention.

The third case is about an institutionalized, severely retarded young man who was also diagnosed as depressed. Although the case did not evolve into psychotherapy, as we classically understand it, improvements were sufficient to maximize institutional services. This illustrates another application of Pre-Therapy.

CATATONIA

Prouty and Kubiak (1988a) describe the application of Pre-Therapy to a catatonic schizophrenic client.[2] The client was a 22-year-old Caucasian male who had had several hospitalizations.

Vignette

The client was one of 13 children. His parents were farmers of Polish ethnicity. His mother had been hospitalized several times for schizophrenic problems. Family observation revealed at least one sibling who, although not hospitalized, displayed psychotic symptoms. The family brought the client to the United States for evaluation. A preliminary observation confirmed that the client was potentially responsive to Pre-Therapy.

According to psychiatric documents, the client had been described as: "mute," "autistic," "catatonic," "making no eye contact," "exhibiting trance-like behavior," "stuporous," "confused," "not establishing rapport," "delusional," "paranoid," and finally, "experiencing severe thought blocking."

He had been diagnosed variously as: manic-depressive, hysterical reaction, hebephrenic schizophrenic, paranoid schizophrenic, catatonic schizophrenic, profound schizophrenic, schizophrenic, affective type. He had received six electro-shock treatments, as well as numerous chemical interventions including Stelazine, Diazepam, Imipramine, Chlorpromazine, Anafranil, Phenothiazine, Haldol, and Trifluoperazine.

The client was returned to his home for several months while plans for residential care and legal details were arranged. My associate therapist arrived and found that the client, kept at home for several months, had deteriorated into psychosis. The parents had not rehospitalized him. He was in a severe catatonic state, having withdrawn to the lower portion of the three-story home. He did not eat meals with the family, only creeping out at night to use the family refrigerator. He had lost considerable weight and his feet were blue from being cramped and stiffened due to his lack of movement and circulation.

The contact work. This vignette describes segments of a 12-hour process that illustrates the application of contact reflections, the successful resolution of the catatonic state, and the development of communicative contact (without medication).

The patient was sitting on a long couch, very rigid, with arms outstretched and even with his shoulders. His eyes were straight ahead, his face was mask-like, and his hands and feet were blue-gray.

The therapist sat on the opposite side of the couch, giving no eye contact to the patient. Reflections were given five to ten minutes apart.

Segment I	(approximately 2:00 P.M.)
Therapist: SR	I can hear the children playing.
Therapist: SR	It is very cool down here.
Therapist: SR	I can hear people talking in the kitchen.
Therapist: SR	I'm sitting with you in the lower level of your house.
Therapist: SR	I can hear the dog barking.
Therapist: BR	Your body is very rigid.
Therapist: BR	You are sitting very still.
Therapist: BR	You are looking straight ahead.
Therapist: BR	You are sitting on the couch in a very upright position.
Therapist: BR	Your body isn't moving. Your arms are in the air.
Client:	[No response, no movement.]

She brought a chair and sat in it directly in front of the patient and mirrored his body exactly as she saw it.

Segment II	**(approximately 3:30 P.M.)**
Therapist: BR	Your body is very rigid. You are sitting on the couch and not moving.
	(approximately 15–20 minutes later)
Therapist:	I can no longer hold my arms outstretched. My arms are tired.
Client:	[No response, no movement.]
Therapist: BR	Your body is very stiff.
Therapist: BR	Your arms are outstretched.
Therapist: BR	Your body isn't moving.
Client:	[Put his hands on his head, as if to hold his head, and spoke in a barely audible whisper.] My head hurts me when my father speaks.
Therapist: WWR	My head hurts me when my father speaks.
Therapist: BR	[Therapist put her hands as if to hold her head.]
Therapist: RR/WW	My head hurts when my father speaks.
Client:	[Continued to hold head for two to three hours.]
Segment III	**(approximately 8:00 P.M.)**
Therapist: SR	It's evening. We are in the lower level of your home.
Therapist: BR	Your body is very rigid.
Therapist: BR	Your hands are holding your head.
Therapist: RR/WW	My head hurts when my father speaks.
Client:	[Immediately dropped his hands to his knees and looked directly into therapist's eyes.]
Therapist: BR	You've taken your hands from your head and placed them on your knees.
	You are looking right into my eyes.
Client:	[Sat motionless for hours.]
Therapist: RR/BR	You dropped your hands from your head to your knees.
Therapist: SR	You are looking straight into my eyes.
Client:	[Immediately, he speaks in a barely audible whisper.] Priests are devils.
Therapist: WWR	Priests are devils.
Therapist: BR	Your hands are on your knees.

Therapist: SR	You are looking right into my eyes.
Therapist: BR	Your body is very rigid.
Client:	[He speaks in a barely audible whisper.] My brothers can't forgive me.
Therapist: WWR	My brothers can't forgive me.
Client:	[Sat motionless for approximately an hour.]

Segment IV　　　　　　　　**(approximately 1:45 A.M.)**

Therapist: SR	It is very quiet.
Therapist: SR	You are in the lower level of the house.
Therapist: SR	It is evening.
Therapist: BR	Your body is very rigid.
Client:	[Immediately, in slow motion, put his hand over his heart and talks.] My heart is wooden.
Therapist: BR/WW	In slow motion, put her hand over her heart and talks.] My heart is wooden.
Client:	[Feet start to move.]
Therapists: BR	Your feet are starting to move.
Client:	[More eye movement.]

The therapist took the patient's hand and lifted him to stand. They began to walk. The patient walked with the therapist around the farm and in a normal conversational mode spoke about the different animals. He brought the therapist to newborn puppies and lifted one to hold. The client had good eye contact. The client continued to maintain communicative contact over the next four days and was able to transfer planes and negotiate with Customs officers on the way to the United States. He was able to sign himself into the residential treatment facility, where he underwent classical Person-Centered/Experiential psychotherapy.

This vignette illustrates the function of Pre-Therapy, which is to restore the client's psychological contact enabling treatment. Very clearly, this client's reality and communicative contact were improved sufficiently to enter psychotherapy.

Pre-Expressive Verbal Communication

It should be reported that apparently meaningless statements, in the psychotic processing, proved to be very germane to the etiology of the psychosis.

"My head hurts when my father speaks": This statement became clarified when anger about physical and emotional abuse emerged in therapy.

"Priests are devils": This meaning became clearer when it was discovered that the family priest made homosexual overtures toward the client. This was the event that precipitated the psychosis.

"My brothers can't forgive me": This referred to a homicidal attempt on his brother's life. The client ran over his brother with a farm tractor. He had a delusional belief that his brother was a Communist.

These non-explicated, out-of-context, highly relevant statements illustrate the pre-expressive nature of psychotic communication.

CRISIS

Prouty and Kubiak (1988b) report the use of Pre-Therapy as a form of crisis intervention. The client was a mentally retarded female, diagnosed as hebephrenic schizophrenic. She lived in a residential treatment facility. The para-professional therapist (now a professional counselor and college instructor) was taking a group of clients on a community visit. The psychotic reaction occurred while they were driving in a van.

The Vignette

The client was one of seven on an outing from a halfway house. She was seated in the rear seat of the van. As I looked in the rear-view mirror, I observed the client crouched down into the seat with one arm outstretched above her head. The client's face was filled with terror and her voice began to escalate in screams.

I pulled the van off the road and asked the volunteer to take the others out of the van. I sat next to the client, sharing the same seat. The client's eyes were closed and she was wincing with fear.

Client:	[In rising voice.] It's pulling me in.
Therapist: WWR	It's pulling me in.
Client:	[Continuing to slip farther down into the seat, with left arm outstretched. Eyes still closed.]
Therapist: BR	Your body is slipping down into the seat. Your arm is in the air.
Therapist: SR	We are in the van. You are sitting next to me.
Client:	[Screaming.]
Therapist: FR	You are screaming, Carol.
Client:	It's pulling me in.
Therapist: WWR	It's pulling you in.
Therapist: SR	Carol, we are in the van. You are sitting next to me.
Therapist: FR	Something is frightening you. You are screaming.
Client:	[Patient screaming.] It's sucking me in.
Therapist: WWR	It's sucking you in.
Therapist: SR/BR	We are in the van, Carol. You are sitting next to me. Your arm is in the air.
Client:	[Beginning to sob very hard. Arms dropped to lap.] It was the vacuum cleaner.
Therapist: WWR	It was the vacuum cleaner.
Client:	[Direct eye contact.] She did it with the vacuum cleaner. [Continued in a normal tone of voice.] I thought it was gone. She used to turn on the vacuum cleaner when I was bad and put the hose right on my arm. I thought it sucked it in. [Less sobbing. It should be noted that daily, this patient would kiss her arm up to her elbow and stroke it continually.]
Therapist: WWR	Your arm is still here. It didn't get sucked into the vacuum cleaner.
Client:	[Smiled and was held by therapist.]

Later that afternoon, a psychotherapy session was held and the client began to delve into her feelings about punishment received as a child. The kissing and stroking of the arm ceased. This vignette illustrates how the client was helped to deal with the acute episode in a psychologically beneficial manner without medications. The client was able to experience how her symptoms of arm kissing and stroking related to a negative childhood emotional trauma of her mother threatening her with a vacuum cleaner. In addition, the client was able to use this newly integrated material as a basis for further therapy concerning her mother.

PROFOUND RETARDATION AND DEPRESSION

Psychiatric treatment of the severely depressed and retarded has been achieved with lithium carbonate (Sovner and Hurley, 1983). Prouty and Cronwall (1990) report a successful psychological treatment utilizing Pre-Therapy.

The Vignette

Client X was a 21-year-old male and a custodial resident of a state institution. He was diagnosed as profoundly retarded on the basis of Stanford Binet testing. His mental age was two years and four months. His IQ was 13.

Because of the severity of symptoms, he was not eligible for vocational or educational training. In addition, he was ineligible for field trips or cottage activities. His symptoms included crying, psychomotor retardation, mood swings, and obsessive stereotypic grass pulling.

Medical records indicate the client had minor cerebral palsy and a history of slow motor development, sitting up at 14 months and walking at 22 months. The parents were of lower socioeconomic status. The father, an alcoholic, physically and emotionally abused the boy during his first five years of life. This resulted in divorce and the boy being placed in the institution. The mother remained in good contact with the youngster and became involved in parent advocacy at the state facility.

The case is significant because the psychological treatment was completed without medications, thus allowing a clearer assessment. The client had previously been treated with Prolixin, Thorazine, Mellaril, and Vistaril. All medications were stopped at the beginning of Pre-Therapy.

As a result of treatment, symptoms decreased and the client exhibited more realistic communication. This increase in realistic communication was confirmed by objective data, and the client became eligible for programmatic services within the institution.

Early Treatment: Autistic Phase—Therapist Report. Treatment sessions were 30 minutes, twice weekly. "During our first sessions, X would come loping into the room, sit down in a chair, and start driving an imaginary car. He would hold his hands and arms as on a steering wheel. (I later introduced a toy steering wheel.) He made clicking noises (turn signals) and engine noises ("Vroom") over and over during the session. He would pretend to turn the wheel and bend sideways until he was touching the floor with his hand, shoulder, or arm. Sometimes he would make great crashing noises and say, "Beep-beep." He drove continually and constantly during sessions for approximately the first year. There was very little eye contact during this time.

Typical Session

Therapist:	Hi, X.
Therapist: SR	You're looking at the steering wheel.
Therapist: SR	X is sitting in the chair, holding the steering wheel.
Therapist: SR	We're both sitting in brown chairs.
Client:	Vroom.
Therapist: WWR	Vroom.
Client:	Click, click.
Therapist: WWR	Click, click.
Therapist: SR	X is turning the steering wheel.
Therapist: BR	Arms crossing. [Crosses arms.]
Therapist: BR	Body bending in chair. [Bends.]
Client:	Vroom, vroom.
Therapist: WWR	Vroom, vroom.
Therapist: SR	Our heads are touching the floor.
Therapist: BR	We are bending over.
Therapist: FR	You are looking.
Therapist: SR	You are looking at the steering wheel.
Client:	Eee, kruss, sss.

Therapist: WWR	Eee, kruss, sss.
Therapist: SR	You're making crashing noises.
Client:	Click, click.
Therapist: WWR	Click, click.
Therapist: SR	You're making signal noises.
Therapist: SR	We're sitting in a big room.
Therapist: SR	The sun is shining.
Therapist: BR	We're facing each other.
Therapist: BR	Your arms are turning.
Therapist: BR	[Hands on steering wheel.]
Therapist: BR	You do, I do.
Therapist: FR	X is smiling.
Therapist: SR	X has been driving for a long time.
Therapist: RR	Last time we were together, we were in a small room.
Therapist: FR	You look sad.
Therapist: SR	You are making crashing sounds.
Therapist: BR	You do, I do.
Client:	Vroom, vroom.
Therapist: WWR	Vroom, vroom.
Client:	Beep, beep.
Therapist: WWR	Beep, beep.
Therapist: RR	Last time we were together, you had a red shirt on.
Therapist: SR	Today you have a yellow shirt.
Client:	Vroom, vroom.
Therapist: WWR	Vroom, vroom.
Client:	Vroom, vroom.
Therapist: WWR	Vroom, vroom.

Mid Treatment: Relatedness Phase—Therapist Report. Gradually, the client became aware that I was reflecting his verbalizations and body movements. As we started to make contact, he would drive, giving me eye contact and smiling as I did contact reflections. He would contort his body so his head was on the floor; however, he was seated in the chair, making driving sounds and actions. He would look to be sure I was giving contact reflections. We spent a lot of time driving, turning corners so that our upper bodies were almost on the floor, while our backsides remained in the chairs.

As the driving behaviors slowly decreased he would play with cars and other toys. I brought a large unbreakable mirror to the sessions. He would make faces into it and simultaneously watch his image while watching my reflections of his facial expressions. We played with a toy whose different shapes fit into holes of the same shape. At first, he played only with the basic toy and he had trouble fitting the shapes successfully. From there he moved to fitting the shapes in easily and then became uninterested in the toy altogether. He liked to draw and continued to enjoy playing with cars. His crying behavior was diminishing in the cottage. During all this time I used only Pre-Therapy contact reflections.

Therapist:	Hi, X.
Client:	Hi, Mimi.
Therapist: SR	You looked at Mindy when you said hi.
Therapist: SR	You sit in chair.
Therapist: SR	You're looking for the steering wheel.
Therapist: FR	You look all around.
Therapist: SR	You picked up steering wheel.
Therapist: FR	You're smiling.
Client:	Vroom, vroom.
Therapist: WWR	Vroom, vroom.
Therapist: FR	You watch Mindy.
Therapist: SR	The big mirror is on the table.
Therapist: FR	You stick out your tongue.
Therapist: RR	You do, I do.
Therapist: FR	You smile when Mindy sticks out her tongue.
Therapist: SR	We are both looking in the mirror.
Therapist: BR	X and Mindy are sitting next to each other.
Therapist: SR	X and Mindy look in the mirror.
Therapist: FR	X smiles.
Therapist: FR	You smile, I smile.
Therapist: FR	Your lips are turned down.
Therapist: SR	You are looking at X in the mirror.

Therapist: FR	X is frowning.
Client:	Here.
Therapist: WWR	Here.
Therapist: FR	Now your lips turned up.
Therapist: FR	You do, I do.
Therapist: FR	X is smiling.
Therapist: SR	You pick up the steering wheel.
Client:	Vroom, vroom.
Therapist: WWR	Vroom, vroom.
Client:	Vroom, vroom.
Therapist: WWR	Vroom, vroom.
Therapist: SR	You look in mirror.
Therapist: RR	You used to drive all the time.
Therapist: SR	Now you drive sometimes.
Therapist: SR	You pick up the red and blue toy.
Therapist: SR	You're turning the toy around in your hands.
Therapist: SR	You hand me the toy.
Client:	Open.
Therapist: FR	You look.
Therapist: FR	You look at Mindy.
Therapist: SR	You want to take the shapes out of the toy.
Therapist: FR	You watch.
Therapist: RR	Last time we were sitting in the chairs.
Therapist: RR	Last time it was raining.
Therapist: SR	Today the sun is shining.
Therapist: RR	Before, X said, "Open."
Client:	Here.
Therapist: WWR	Here.
Therapist: SR	You want the triangle in the hole.
Therapist: FR	X smiles.
Therapist: BR	You do, I do.

Ending Treatment: Expressive Phase—Therapist Report. In the ending phase of therapy, X's driving behavior was extinct, as was his crying behavior. He no longer tore up the grass and he took part in a pre-vocational program. He went home from our sessions without the aid of staff. During our sessions he was more verbal and more assertive, expressing higher self-esteem. He would walk around the room and ask basic questions. He would express emotions appropriately and knew when he was happy or sad. He was able to attend field trips. He would even talk about other people, showing much improved reality contact and social communication.

Therapist:	Hi, X.
Client:	Fine.
Therapist:	How are you today?
Client:	Fine.
Therapist: WWR	Fine.
Therapist: SR	You're taking off your coat.
Therapist: SR	You are looking at Mindy.
Client:	Hang up?
Therapist: WWR	Hang up?
Therapist: SR	You want to know what to do with your coat. You can put it over there.
Therapist: SR	You put your coat on the chair.
Therapist: SR	You're walking across the room.
Therapist: BR	You sit down.
Therapist: SR	You put your arms on the table.
Therapist: BR	You do, I do.
Therapist: SR	You reach in the bag.
Therapist: SR	X takes out the green car.
Client:	Vroom, vroom.
Therapist: WWR	Vroom, vroom.
Therapist: SR	X pushes the car off the table.
Therapist: SR	It flies across the room.
Therapist: FR	X laughs.
Therapist: BR	X stands up.
Therapist: SR	X pushes chair back.
Therapist: SR	X picks up car.
Therapist: SR	You're walking to the candy machine.

Therapist: SR	You're rattling the handle.
Client:	Candy.
Therapist: WWR	Candy.
Client:	Candy (louder).
Therapist: WWR	Candy.
Therapist: SR	X wants candy.
Therapist: SR	No candy now, X.
Therapist: SR	You're looking at Mindy.
Therapist: BR	You're walking.
Therapist: SR	You're looking at the stuff on the counter.
Client:	Plates.
Therapist: WWR	Plates.
Client:	Napkins.
Therapist: WWR	Napkins.
Client:	Party?
Therapist: WWR	Party.
Therapist: SR	You want to know if there is going to be a party?
Therapist: SR	Christmas is coming.
Client:	Santa.
Therapist: WWR	Santa.
Therapist: SR	Santa comes at Christmas.
Therapist:	What are you doing for Christmas?
Client:	Going home in car.
Therapist: WWR	Going home in car.
Client:	See Mom.
Therapist: WWR	See Mom.
Therapist: RR	You'll see Mom when you go home for Christmas.
Therapist: RR	Before you laughed when you pushed the car off the table.
Therapist: FR	You smiled when Mindy says that.
Therapist:	Is someone coming to take you back to your house?
Client:	No.
Therapist:	Good-bye, X.
Client:	Good-bye, Mimi.

A four-year follow-up review showed a stabilized and improved adjustment. The client was still without psychiatric medications. Institutional records indicate the client's accessibility to programmatic services. He participates in vocational, educational, and social activities. However, records also indicate instances of crying and verbal aggression.

An interview with his mother revealed her impressions: "He's improved a lot. . . . I really think it helped him a lot. . . . We can bring him home now for longer periods of time without as much stress. . . . It worked great."

Most interestingly, she reported, "It helped him see himself." His mother also wished the treatment could have continued longer if circumstances could have permitted.

NOTES

1. Ms. Pietrzak served as Pre-Therapy pilot study coordinator. She had primary responsibility for organizing and supervising the project.

2. This case history was presented at a symposium with Carl Rogers, Eugene Gendlin, Natalie Rogers, and Nathaniel Raskin at the University of Chicago in September 1986. The videotape is available at the Institute for the Study of the Person, La Jolla, California.

Part III

EVOLUTIONS IN EXPERIENTIAL THEORY

Chapter 7

The Pre-Symbolic Structure and Experiencing of Schizophrenic Hallucinations

HISTORICAL INTRODUCTION

Hallucinations have played a significant role in the history of Christian theology and early psychiatric thought (Sarbin and Juhass, 1967).

In A.D. 354, St. Augustine evaluated visions in terms of their mystical validity, or their closeness to or remoteness from worldly origins. He considered it important to discern whether a vision was corporeal (real, with time and space referents). If the vision was judged to be imagined, it had little spiritual value; if it was judged intellectual (seen in the mind's eye), it was considered a step in spiritual progress.

Thomas Aquinas (A.D. 1226) examined visions in the light of natural or supernatural origins. If deemed of a supernatural source, the vision was either from God or from the devil. If the vision was of the devil, the person was accused of heresy or witchcraft, with the possibility of being burned alive at the stake.

Moving toward a more benign interpretation, St. Teresa of Avila (A.D. 1515) was the first to suggest that some visions could be derived from natural causes in the form of sickness. Visions, she thought, could come from melancholia, weak imaginations, drowsiness, sleep, or sleep-like states. The distinction over their origin was fundamental for protecting people from the Inquisition and enabling a transfer from ecclesiastical authorities to physicians.

Under the medical concept, Galen's theory of insanity distinguished between melancholia and mania. Both were caused by "black bile" (a medical belief of this historical period), which was considered to have injurious effects on mental functions.

The word "hallucination" first appears in English in the writings of Lavater (A.D. 1572) who wrote: "Ghosts and spriites walking by nyte, and strange noyeses, cracks, and sundry forwaranyes, which commonly happen before the death of menns, great slaughters and alterations of Kyngdomes." Hallucinations meant a wandering of mind.

During the eighteenth century, Battie further defined the hallucination by declaring that the seer must be unalterably convinced of the existence of the unreal image. Chrieton introduced the term "hallucination" into formal medical language. Esquirol distinguished in the nineteenth century between hallucination and illusion. Hallucinations were from the brain, while illusions were considered perceptual mistakes.

In the last half of the nineteenth century, hallucinations were romanticized through the writings of great literary figures such as Edgar Allan Poe (alcohol), Samuel Taylor Coleridge (nitrous oxide), Thomas De Quincy (opium), Arthur Rimbaud (hashish), and Nathaniel Hawthorne (dream-like states).

In the beginning of the twentieth century, Sigmund Freud interpreted hallucinations as psychopathological and structurally similar to dreams as psychic projections. He combined them under the common rubric of "primary process." This set the stage for modern psychological approaches to viewing hallucinations.

PRE-SYMBOLIC THEORY

The Problematic

As previously indicated in Chapter 3, Gendlin (1964) describes hallucinations as "structure-bound" Experiencing. The concept of structure-bound contains several levels of meaning. First, hallucinations are perceived literally by the client "as such" and as "not his." Second, the particular structure-bound experience is isolated. The experiencing is not included in the felt functioning of the organism. Third, this implicitly felt functioning is rigid, not in experiential process. This isolation and rigidity results in a loss of self-sense. Finally, structure-bound is a static, repetitious, and an unmodifiable mode of Experiencing.

Clearly, hallucinations are conceptualized by Gendlin as structure-bound—or, one may say, as a *non-process structure*. This presents a theoretical problem. As I have stated in Chapter 3, experiential process is the essence of therapeutic change, yet it is the element that is impaired or absent. Gendlin's phenomenological description of hallucinatory structure-bound "state" yields the problematic of how to turn a non-process structure into a process structure.

The Primacy of the Symbol

The shift from a non-process structure to a process structure involves an epistemic shift from phenomenology to the primacy of the symbol. This primacy of the symbol, in human nature, is asserted by Cassirer (1955), who described humankind as "Animal Symbolicum." Essentially, humans are conceived as symbolic animals. The vast super-structure of culture, language, arts, science, religion, philosophy, and so on are thought of as symbolization.

This philosophical impulse is given further articulation by Langer (1961), who describes the human brain as a "transformer." The brain transforms "the current of experience into symbols." This metaphor allows us to think of humankind in an essential way as motivated to symbolize experience.

Semiotics

The multiple ways in which humans symbolize their experience is described by the science of semiotics.

Reichenbach (Szasz, 1961) outlines levels of symbolizing experience in terms of abstractness or concreteness. The most abstract form of symbolizing experience is the meta-symbol. Meta-symbols are exemplified by scientific symbols; for example, $E = MC^2$. This symbol does not refer to an experience, but to a set of processes beyond direct experience. Another example for the meta-symbol is Christianity: No one can experience all of Christianity. The symbols of logic are still another example of meta-symbol. These symbols refer to other symbols and not to lived experience. Meta-symbols are extremely abstract.

The next level of symbolizing experience is object-language. Object-language is ordinary cultural speech. This level of abstractness is described by the function of a word that refers to a concrete. For example, the word "book" refers to the physical object. The word "cow" refers to the literal animal.

Continuing along the abstractness and concreteness continuum is the indexical sign. The indexical sign is a concrete experience that refers to a concrete experience. For example, in nature the concrete storm cloud refers to the concrete rain. The perspiration of a person refers to the hot sun.

An even more concrete form of symbolizing experience is the iconic sign. An iconic sign is a literal duplicate of the referent. This is exemplified by the photographic picture or the phonographic record. These are exact copies of their referent; they are symbolic duplicates.

An even more primitive form of concreteness is the pre-symbol (Prouty, 1986). It "cannot be clarified by something else" and "it is inseparable from what it symbolizes" (Jaspers, 1971).

The Meaning of Pre-Symbol

The term "pre-symbol" refers to the structure of a hallucinatory image, as distinct from its processing. Psychotherapy with schizophrenic clients reveals that the hallucinatory image contains properties that are both phenomenological and symbolic. This creates a definitional polarity.

Sartre (1956) described the phenomenon as an experience that is "absolutely self-indicative." This means an experience indicates itself, refers to itself, or means itself.

Whitehead (1927) described a symbol as "an experience that indicates another experience." This means symbols are experiences that indicate other experiences—that an experience refers to another experience, or that an experience means another experience.

In essence, the phenomenon is an "about itself," and the symbol is an "about something else." The co-existence of these two polarities requires a synthesis to fully describe the structural reality of the hallucination. This is the foundation for the term "pre-symbol."

Theoretical Concepts

The hallucination as pre-symbol exhibits three attributes or properties: expressive, phenomenological, and symbolic.

Expressive. As an expressive structure, the hallucination is described as "self-intentional." As stated earlier, Langer (1961) views the human brain as a "transformer" that transforms the *current of experience* into symbols. This motivational metaphor allows us to think of the hallucination as an expressive transformation of real-life experience into image form.

One client described the essence of this self-intentionality, saying, "These images are my unconscious trying to express itself."

Another client described it as "the past trying to come back."

Still another conveyed this volitional quality by saying, "The images start in my unconscious and move toward my consciousness to become real."

Phenomenological. As a phenomenological structure, the hallucination is described as "self-indicating." It is experienced as real, and as such, it implies itself. Experience A implies experience A. Thus, the hallucination *means itself as itself.*

Symbolic. As a symbolic structure, the hallucination is described as "self-referential." As a symbol, it is an experience that implies another experience. Experience A implies experience B. The hallucinatory image (experience A) contains its referent (experience B) within itself. The hallucinatory image *means itself within itself.*

As psychological fact, do hallucinations concretely manifest the properties of being self-intentional, self-indicating, and self-referential?

PRE-SYMBOLICS: DISCOVERY-ORIENTED PSYCHOTHERAPY

Mahrer (1992) describes the difference between hypothesis-oriented psychotherapy research and discovery-oriented psychotherapy. The former is concerned with research design and statistical assessment, the latter with clinical discovery. This discovery approach is illustrated by Boss (1963, 1980), who found hallucinations to be significant in the psychotherapy of schizophrenia.

The major discovery of Pre-Symbolic psychotherapy is that schizophrenic hallucinatory experiencing leads to the integration of reality-based "not-conscious" experiences.

Pre-Symbolic Experiencing I

Pre-Symbolic Experiencing I (Prouty, 1991) is deeply rooted in the Rogerian approach and illustrates the self-intentional, self-indicating, and self-referential properties of the hallucinations.

The Client. The client, a male aged 19, was diagnosed as moderately retarded (Stanford-Binet IQ of 65). He was from upper-lower class origins of Polish ethnicity. There was no mental illness in the family of origin, and the client had not been diagnosed or treated for mental illness; that is, he was not receiving any medications for psychosis. He was a day-client in a vocational rehabilitation workshop for the mentally retarded. He was referred to me for therapy because of severe withdrawal and non-communicativeness. The client also behaved as though he was very frightened. He was shaking and trembling at his work station and during his bus ride to the facility. At home, he rarely talked with his parents and he never socialized with neighborhood peers.

During the early phases of therapy, the client expressed almost nothing and made very little contact with me. He was very frightened during the sessions and could barely tolerate being in the same room. Gradually, with the aid of contact reflections, the client accepted a minimal relationship and expressed himself in a minimal way.

Eventually, it became clear the client was terrorized by hallucinations that were constantly present to him.

The following description provides an account of Pre-Symbolic Experiencing. It provides an outline of hallucinatory movement and its subsequent resolution about its origins. The first phase describes a purple, demonic, evil appearance that "hangs there" above the client. The second phase describes an orange, square image with anger "in it." This had a profound frightening effect on the client. The third phase presents a woman with orange hair and green eyes. She is both pretty and helpful—also mean and bad. It also contains the active recapturing of a real-life experience in which the retarded client was beaten by a nun because he did not understand his lessons in school.

Phase I: "Purple Demon"

Client:	It's very evil, this thing. What it wants to do is to rip me apart, you know. It's very evil . . . and it's very evil, this thing. It wants to rip me apart, but it's very evil, this thing. That's why I don't want anything to do with it. I'm tempted by it, you know. It's so small, but it has so much strength and it wants to rip me apart, you know. It wants to drive me into the past. It wants . . . it wants to make the past come back and I don't want the past to come back like it did a long time ago. It's over with, you know. It's not coming back anymore. The past doesn't come back, it's over with already.
Therapist:	It's evil and strong. It wants the past to come back.
Client:	This evil thing is a picture. It's a purple picture that hangs there. It just hangs and I can see it. I can see it . . . the picture, you know. It's purple, it's very dark. It's very dark. So I can see it and I don't like it. I don't like it at all. It's very dark.
Therapist:	It's a dark purple picture and you don't like it.
Client:	And . . . it's very tempted and I don't want to be tempted by it. It's very small. It's very evil, you know . . . that's all. . . . It just hangs there. It don't do nothing. It's very evil. It's tempted. I'm tempted by it and it's very evil, you know. It's just like a picture. A purple picture. It just stays there. It just stays there, you know, the picture. . . . It don't do nothing, it's evil, you know. I don't like it at all. It's not good and this thing, whatever it is. It's in the past and it's very strong, the past. . . . And it's over with and it's not coming back anymore. The past doesn't come back, and this is like now. It ain't the past, you know. It's over with and I don't want to be tempted by it anymore. Yeh, yeh . . . it's very evil, very evil and very strong and has a lot of strength to it.
Therapist:	It's evil and it's in the past. It's strong and it hangs there. You don't want to be tempted by it.

Client: This thing, you know . . . this thing has a very lot of
               strength to it. It's evil, you know. This thing has a very lot
               of strength to it. It's evil. It's not good and that's why it's
               not good at all. It's very evil, you know. I don't like it. It's
               very evil, this thing [pained laughter]. It's over with. It's
               the past, and it's not coming back anymore. It's over with
               a long time ago, you know. It's not going to come back
               anymore. I used to talk about the trees and the flowers,
               grass, and it's all over with. It's not coming back anymore.
               It's something else, the picture. The purple picture just
               hangs there. It's evil. No?

Therapist: The purple picture just hangs there. It's evil and you don't
               like it.

Client: The past, it came from the past and the past is over with.
               It's not coming back anymore, you know.

Therapist: It comes from the past.

Client: It's a picture. It's just a picture. A big purple picture. It just
               hangs there. . . . I don't think it will rip me apart. I think it's
               very strong, but it ain't going to rip me apart, I don't think
               it will rip me apart at all, no.

Therapist: It's a big purple picture. It won't rip you apart.

Client: This thing is getting big and large. It's very big and large.
               It wants to get me. I won't let it. It's evil. It's like a demon,
               a bad demon. It wants to chop me all up. I won't let it chop
               me all up because it's bad. Very bad [loud sobs]. Just a
               temptation, like any other temptation. A temptation is a
               temptation. You shouldn't be tempted by it and you know
               I want to pull away from it. I don't want to go by it.

Therapist: It's big and large and evil. It wants to chop you. It's very
               tempting.

Client: It's very bad and it's very destructive. It ain't good at all by
               it. It's like a bad demon, like a . . . like a demon devil or
               something. Like a demon devil and I don't care for it too
               much. You know, at all. I . . . I don't like it too much, no. I
               don't like it at all, this thing. It's very bad and very evil,
               you know. It ain't no good. It's very bad. It's with the past
               and it's not going to come back anymore. It's over with,
               you know, and talking about the trees and the flowers and
               grass and that's over. I mean, it's not coming back, but this
               is right now, I mean.

Therapist: It's bad and destructive, like a demon devil. It's evil and with the past.

Client: It's not coming back, but this is right here now. I can feel it, you know. It's like air. It's up above me. It's very up above and I can feel . . . almost touch it, you know. It's so close, very close. It's like a demon, you know, demon devil or something. "Ho, ho, hoing" and all like that, you know . . . very bad, very bad. It forces me, pressing, very pressing on me. . . . It's very pressing, it forces, a lot of force to it and it wants to grab me, you know. It wants to grab me. The feeling wants to grab me. The feeling wants to grab me.

Therapist: It's very close and it wants to grab you.

Client: The feeling . . . the feeling . . . ah, it's in the picture. The feeling is in the picture. Yes, it's there and I can see it. I don't like it. It's over with, you know. It's like the past and it's not coming back anymore. It's over. It's just the trees and flowers and grass and that's over and it's not coming back.

Phase I describes a purple demonic image that just "hangs there." The client experiences it as evil and powerful. The image is considered destructive and it wants to rip the client apart.

This phase contains the property of being self-intentional. The client expresses: "It wants to drive me into the past" and *It wants to make the past come back* and I don't want the past to come back like it did a long time ago. . . . It's over with, you know. . . . It's not coming back anymore. . . . The past doesn't come back, it's over already. . . . *It's in the past and it's very strong*, the past and it's over with and it's not coming back anymore. . . . The past doesn't come back and this is like now. . . . It ain't the past, you know. . . . It's over with and I don't want to be tempted by it. . . . It's the past and it's not coming back anymore."

As illustrated by this example, "self-intentional" means the expressive transformation of real-life experiences into images.

Phase II: "Orange Square Hate"

Client: It's orange, the color's in a square. It's an orange color that's square and it hates me. And it don't even like me. It hates me.

Therapist: It's orange and it's square and it hates you.

Client:	It hates me a lot, you know, and it scares me. I get scared because of that. I get scared because it hates me.
Therapist:	It's orange and it's square and you get scared a lot.
Client:	And because it's orange, that scares me and I get scared of the bad hating.
Therapist:	The orange and bad hating scare you a lot. That hate scares you.
Client:	I get scared because of that. I get scared a lot. I get scared of the orange thing. It's orange.
Therapist:	You get scared of the orange thing.
Client:	Big orange, square thing. It's square and it's orange and I hate it. It don't like me because it hates me. It hates me and I get scared and I get excited over it too. I get very excited.
Therapist:	You get very excited.
Client:	It's exciting, I'm excited over it too. I do, I do. I get excited over it a lot. What? I get scared a lot about it. It makes noises. It makes noises.
Therapist:	It's orange and it makes noises.
Client:	It makes noises. . . . It hates me. It also gets me excited. It gets me excited. It does, it gets me very excited a lot. I get, I get, I get very excited over it. I do, I do. I do. There's so much hate and it scares me and it makes me uncomfortable. It does. And it's real. . . . It's real, it is.
Therapist:	It's real.
Client:	It is, it's very real.
Therapist:	It's very real. . . . You point to it. It's over on your side. You see it.
Client:	I see it. Over there, over there.
Therapist:	It's over there.
Client:	It makes sounds, too.

Phase II has an image that is orange, square, and has hate in it. The client is very frightened of it. Phase II contains self-indicating properties because it is experienced as real, as a phenomenon. It implies itself. The client's process is as follows: "*and it's real,* it is. . . . *It is, it's very real.* . . . I see it. . . . Over there. . . . Over there. . . . It makes sounds, too."

Phase III: "Mean Lady"

Client:	Yeah, well. Yeah, I would. I would. She's . . . I don't know. There we go. What? What? [Audio hallucination.]
Therapist:	Okay, let's talk about what you see.
Client:	Well, she ain't real, you know, and she ain't real, you know. What? [Audio hallucination.] Ha ha ha. [Sobs.] She has orange hair and yellow eyes.
Therapist:	She has orange hair and yellow eyes.
Client:	She's very pretty. She's very pretty. She loves getting mean when I am bad. She could get . . . she's mean, you know.
Therapist:	She's pretty.
Client:	She's also mean, too. She can be mean if I'm bad. The possibility of the mean scares me. It does scare me a lot over that.
Therapist:	She's pretty and mean.
Client:	She is. She is. No, really she is. Really she is—with yellow eyes and orange hair. Boy! That scares me. That scares me a lot. That scares me a lot. . . . Yeah, both the meanness and the . . . What? [Audio hallucination.] Yeah. Aah, I can see it and I don't even want to see it. It's over with and it's not coming back anymore. I can even see it.
Therapist:	You can see it.
Client:	Yeah, that scares me. Yeah, it does. I think about it. I think it scares me.
Therapist:	When you think about it, that scares you.
Client:	I get scared. I don't want to think about it. I got it. I got it.
Therapist:	You don't want to think about it, but you got it.
Client:	I got it. It's orange, you know. That's helping, she's helping.
Therapist:	She's helping.
Client:	She scares me though, she scares me. But as long as I'm good, but as long as I'm good, I am . . . she's a friend.
Therapist:	As long as you're good, she's a friend.
Client:	But she's scary.
Therapist:	She's scary.
Client:	Scary. Yellow eyes, orange hair she has, she does. Reminds me of a dragon, you know. Her eyes are like that.
Therapist:	Her eyes are like a dragon.

Client:	Almost, you know, like a dragon. . . . Her eyes are like a dragon. . . . She's strong. . . . She's strong, I'm weak. And I'm good, but she's also mean. She can be mean, too, see? And I'm good, if I'm good and I am. I really am, but she's all . . . she's very mean. She can be mean . . . and it scares me.
Therapist:	She's mean and that scares you.
Client:	She looks over me. She watches over me, but she has eyes like a dragon. . . . Right. That's like a dragon and then she scares me and I get scared.

At this point, the client appeared upset and wanted the tape recorder turned off. Over the next two sessions, the image processed into a nun who had beaten the retarded client because he did not understand his school lessons.

Phase III contains an image of a woman that the client describes as pretty, mean, and scary. She has orange hair and yellow eyes. This deeply frightens the client. The significant theoretical observation of this phase is its processing to its "originary" experience. The client recaptures a real memory of being beaten by a nun who punished him for not completing his school lessons. This phase illustrates the self-referential property of hallucinations; that is, it symbolizes an experience within itself. It refers to an "originating" event (the nun).

Pre-Symbolic Experiencing II

Pre-Symbolic Experiencing II (Prouty, 1977) details a description of the hallucination as a process structure.[1] These several vignettes of several clients describe stages of Pre-Symbolic Experiencing in the form of a process typology. These stages of experiencing parallel and further validate the "process conception of psychotherapy" (Rogers, 1961). The hallucination moves from "a fixity and remoteness" of self-experience to "a clear, alive, immediate and integrated" self-experience. The stages of hallucinatory experiencing are described as: (1) the self-indicating stage; (2) the self-emotive stage; (3) the self-processing stage; and (4) the self-integrating stage.

Self-indicating stage. This stage displays a hallucinatory image that signifies itself: It implies and refers to its own existence. It draws attention. The hallucinatory image has empirical signifiers that stand forth and appear energized, that possess some intensity of color or shape or movement.

I see the upper left corner of a square. The lines are yellow—like a bright light shining through the navy blue. The navy blue is so dark it is almost black. The lines sway around, left to right, forward and backward. There is no pattern in the movement.

During the self-indicating stage, the therapeutic technique needs to be directed toward the image itself. Such a focus is desirable in order to make the primary process more perceptually stable and, hence, more accessible to client and therapist. Such technique is labeled "image reflecting."

Image reflecting refers to the reflection of literal, self-indicating properties of the image or symbol itself. In the previous examples, the following imagistic properties would be reflected:

1. Like a bright light shining
2. Is so dark
3. The lines sway around, left to right, forward and backward.

During the self-indicating stage, the hallucination is mostly symbolic, and little manifest affect is present. To initiate the development of feeling, it is necessary to maximize the interactive effect of reflecting and experiencing. It may be necessary to repeat image reflections over and over before feelings begin to emerge from the hallucination.

Self-emotive stage. At this point, affect has developed in or around the hallucinatory image as part of its own self-signification or as a result of reiteration:

It's like a painting. Like a picture painting on the wall, or a painting with feelings—it's like a painting on the wall, only with feelings in it. (Prouty, 1966)

Reflecting in the self-emotive stage is toward both the image and the feeling in order to maintain "process unity" (Gendlin, 1964). If either image or feeling is over-reflected or under-reflected, the total process will split, and the client will experience either a proliferation of images with little feeling, or a density of affect with no emotional process. In the example cited, the therapist would reflect, "It's like a painting" (image) and, "There are feelings in it" (feeling).

In another example, the client's hallucination is "square orange, with anger in it." The therapist would reflect "square orange" (image), and, "There is anger in it" (feeling). If both the image and feeling are reflected and reiterated, both will evolve and process unity will be maintained.

Self-processing stage. During this stage, both image and affect process, and there is a shift from symbolic (image) to non-symbolic experiencing (feelings).

I'm crying huddled in a chair. Garry comes by and I hold on to him. I am afraid. The object has changed from the corner of a square to a head on a stick. It's a man's head. There is a cape on a stick. It is suspended in air. It moves close and then goes back. God, I can't stand it. He—no, it couldn't be true, please, anything but this—he—no—no—no, he didn't do it to me, Lord, not my dad. I loved him. He—he—no, I won't believe it—he tried to kill me.

In the example cited, symbolic and emotional processes are illustrated, as well as the sequential and proportional shift from symbolic content to feeling content:

Symbolic (image) process and content:

1. The object has changed from the corner of a square to a head on a stick.
2. It's a man's head.
3. There is a cape.
4. It moves back and forth.

Feeling process and content:

1. Can't stand it.
2. Can't be true.
3. Please—he didn't.
4. Not my dad.
5. I loved him.
6. I won't believe it.
7. He tried to kill me.

In the self-processing stage, reflections begin to proportionally change from the reiterative-symbolic modality to a more classic Client-Centered concern with feeling. This change is caused by an evolution from a "fixity and remoteness of experience to a clear, alive, immediate, integrated experience" (Rogers, 1961). In essence, there is a shift from symbolic experiencing (image) to non-symbolic experiencing (feeling), and the reflective modality changes along with it.

Self-integrating stage. In this stage, affect shifts from the hallucinatory image to the person's own sense of self, and is integrated, owned, and experienced as self.

It was at this point that the image was no longer merely an external story, but very rapidly I realized that the child was myself. It was impossible to hold back the flow of feeling accompanying the image. It was like being one's self and staring at one's self in the same instant. I felt the fright the child in the image was experiencing.

At this point, reflections are generally much more focused on the feeling process. Since the patient has assimilated and integrated the ego-alien hallucinations, the therapist can shift to traditional Client-Centered/Experiential responses.

Pre-Symbolic Experiencing III

Pre-Symbolic Experiencing III (Prouty and Pietrzak, 1988) describes the application of the Pre-Therapy technique (contact reflections) to the hallucinatory experience.

"Michael," a divorced man in his 60s, was referred as an outpatient. His original diagnosis was phobic-neurosis; however, the referring psychiatrist described the client as experiencing an acute depressive episode and was concerned over possible hospitalization for a developing schizophrenic psychosis. The client was not receiving medication. Presenting symptoms were intense, vivid images that the client periodically experienced as real. Corresponding physical problems were sweating, increased blood pressure, tremors, and other physical manifestations of anxiety. Frequently, these symptoms rendered the client non-functional. These symptoms occurred after the client married his "common-law" wife of several years. The client reported no such symptomology during 30 years of previous marriage or during other intimate relationships.

Michael experienced images of being drowned, and of persons without faces being hurt. He reported feelings of being in a dangerous situation that he could not explain.

Client:	It's like I'm drowning.
Therapist: WWR	You're drowning.
Client:	Yeah.
Therapist: RR	It's like you're drowning.
Client:	Can't figure it—where I am.
Therapist: FR	Where are you? Your face is twisted.
Client:	Where—it's horrible.
Therapist: BR	It's horrible, you're moving all over.
Client:	It's like I'm drowning. Yes, it's me.
Therapist: WWR	It's you.
Client:	It's me drowning. It's not big, it's a bathtub or something.
Therapist: WWR	It's you—bathtub or something.
Client:	I can't breathe. [Client, hands to throat.]
Therapist: BR	It's choking you. [Therapist, hands to throat.]
Client:	It's all over—faces, it's all over.
Therapist: WWR	It's all over.
Client:	Black clear people.
Therapist: WWR	Black clear people.
Client:	Cold. It's getting me.
Therapist: WWR	Cold. It's getting me.
(RR)	It's all over.
Client:	It's me in a bathtub. Faces. I'm in a bathtub.
Therapist: WWR	You're in a bathtub. [Long pause.]
Client:	I'm in a bathtub. I'm drowning. Faces, people, are they getting hurt?
Therapist: WWR	It's you in a bathtub.
Client:	It's me—what's happening? It's getting me. I'm drowning. The faces are ugly.
Therapist: BR	You turn away. You're drowning—ugly.

Client:	It's getting me.
Therapist: WWR	It's getting you.
Client:	It's those faces.
Therapist: WWR	It's those faces, ugly.
Client:	They're mad and black.
Therapist: WWR	They're mad and black.
Client:	I'm drowning. [Client cries.] It's only one.
Therapist: FR	You're crying. You're drowning. It's only one.
Client:	It's smothering me. There is no water in the tub.
Therapist: WWR	It's smothering you. No water.
Client:	No water—the face is smothering me. [Client cries more. Long pause.]
Therapist: WWR	No water—the face is smothering you. You're crying.
Client:	It's my ex-wife. She is smothering me. [Long pause.] Oh, I'm in the basement.
Therapist: WWR	I'm in the basement.
Client:	Help me. [Client sobs.]
Therapist: WWR	It's your ex-wife.
(RR)	You're in the basement.
Client:	Yeah, it's cold and dark.
Therapist: WWR	It's cold and dark.
Client:	My bed is in the corner. It's small.
Therapist: WWR	My bed is in the corner. It's small.
Client:	I sleep in the basement. My marriage smothered me.
Therapist: WWR	My marriage smothered me.
(FR)	You looked pained, eyes big.
Client:	Yeah, I hurt. My marriage smothered me. It's like I was drowning in the relationship.
Therapist: WWR	You're hurting, the marriage was smothering. Your relationship was like drowning.
Client:	All those years I was suffocating because of our wedding vows. We couldn't get a divorce because we were Catholic. Being married again is being tied to those horrible memories of our marriage and religion.
Therapist: WWR	Marriage is horrible because of vows.

Client:	I can't be married. I'm afraid of being suffocated and being lost at sea.
Therapist: WWR	I can't be married. I'm afraid of being suffocated and being lost at sea.
Client:	It took forever for an annulment before. I can't live forever like that again.
Therapist: WWR	It took forever for an annulment before. I can't live forever like that again.
Therapist: FR	You stopped crying.
Client:	I don't know how to be married right. When I go to bed, I remember the nights in the basement. Oh God, they were horrible.

Later, Michael started dealing with issues relating to his past and current marriage. He had gained insight into how his past marriage affected his current marriage. The hallucinations ceased.

Pre-Symbolic Experiencing IV

Pre-Symbolic Experiencing IV (Prouty, 1983) evolved from Gestalt and Experiential concepts. The method is described in three stages: contact, integration, and assimilation.

Phenomenological contact. Perls (1976) describes the "Me" and "Not Me" experience as a contact boundary. The hallucination can be described as a three-dimensional structure with a space serving as a boundary between "Me" and "Not Me." This spatiality is a contact boundary that can be used as a point of contact between self and hallucination.

Phenomenological integration. With a literal contact between self and hallucination, a dramatic integration of the hallucination occurs, presenting what Polster and Polster (1974) describe as a "contact episode."

Phenomenological assimilation. As part of the integration process, the client needs a more gradual assimilation of the experience so that it can become an aspect of the "self-sense" (Gendlin, 1964). This can be achieved by experiential reflections (Gendlin, 1968).

The Client

The client was a woman diagnosed as paranoid schizophrenic with homicidal and suicidal impulses. She was non-medicated and attended outpatient psychotherapy twice weekly for several years. The client had been hallucinating for several months of a huge, coiled, and menacing python. The python would be present in the morning when she put her feet on the floor arising from her bed. The client related that it was present in the rear seat of her automobile as she was driving to therapy. The snake was experienced as coiled into a figure-eight, lying between the client and therapist during sessions.

Therapy Experience

Developing contact. The snake was coiled between the therapist and the client. If the client moved close to the python, it would raise its head in a menacing fashion. Since the python appeared in three-dimensional space, it was mutually decided to walk around it to find a perimeter of psychological safety for the client. This process took several sessions.

The perimeter of psychological safety for the client was a half-circle that arched between the client's and therapist's chairs. This half-circle was a literal dividing line between "psychotic space" (three-dimensional python hallucination) and "sane space" (an area that was hallucination-free). The half-circle functioned as the contact boundary.

Contact was developed by having the client and therapist jointly walk the semi-circle together. Gradually, the client learned to develop a contact gradient. She would walk farther away from and then closer to the contact boundary half-circle. This would allow her to experiment with her experiencing. Moving closer to the contact point would produce more menacing writhing by the snake. She would react by increased trembling, sweating, gasping, loss of bladder control—that is, terror reactions. She would also experience a fever. There was some concern for her physiological safety. This work was only possible because of the deep closeness of a Person-Centered relationship and the client's drive to get well.

Gradually, the client became skilled at controlling her own contact capacities. This client's autonomy and self-directedness were respected She learned to approach the hallucination and increase her capacity to tolerate stressful feelings.

Integrative contact episode. During a mutually agreed single session, the client integrated the hallucination by making direct contact with this three-dimensional image of a python. The integration was achieved by walking with the client and approaching the half-circle contact boundary, and literally entering the psychotic (hallucinatory) space. The snake reared and sunk his teeth into the client. At this point the client screamed at the therapist: "You betrayed me—not you too!" and proceeded to confuse me with her mother (good mother, bad mother).

I became concerned that a psychotic transference had occurred and that the client would become more psychotic and isolated from a therapeutic relationship. This did not occur. The client continued to experientially process. She reached the clarity that the snake was her homicidal mother.

Assimilation. The client slowly assimilated the meaning of the newly integrated experiences by Experiential Processing (Gendlin, 1968). The assimilation phase followed the contact episode almost immediately—within 24 hours. Newly integrated experiences, although viewed as real, often do not have a self-sense quality. The meaning of the newly integrated experience is not "worked through."

By experiential reflections (Gendlin, 1968), the client clarified the following:

A. This is my psychotic split. The snake (action and parts) are my not acknowledged experiences. I retained the beautiful aspects of my mother and denied her homicide.

B. I had to go crazy—not to go crazy. I had to deny being a murder object of my mother.

C. The snake felt like my mother's kill wish. Now I know she really wanted to kill me.

Shortly thereafter, the hallucination shrank in size and dimension; the image relocated to between her mother's breasts, lost realism and intensity, and faded away.

Pre-Symbolic Experiencing: Theoretical Discussion

Pre-Symbolic Experiencing has theoretical implications for Experiential, Gestalt, and Person-Centered psychotherapy. It also has implications for the structure of schizophrenia and as an approach to the unconscious.

The Experiential approach. Pre-Symbolic Experiencing leads to bodily felt experiencing. Pre-Symbolic Experiencing "restores" bodily felt experiencing.

These clinical facts necessitate the redefinition of Experiencing from bodily felt process to include Pre-Symbolic felt process. These concepts find unity as felt process, but differentiate through an epistemic shift from bodily phenomenology to hallucinatory symbology.

The Gestalt approach. The Gestalt approach views the dream as a self-fragment. Analogously, the hallucination can be conceived as a self-fragment. The hallucination parallels the dream as a self-fragment to be integrated.

Viewing the hallucination as a self-fragment permits the description of hallucinatory experience as a severe split in the self-structure—in the language of R. D. Laing, a "divided self" (Spinelli, 1989).

The severe split between self and self-fragment leads to the formulation of language to characterize this divided self. The term "extrojection" can be applied to describe this traumatic rending.

Extrojection is distinguished from projection. The dream (projection) is experienced phenomenologically as "mine." It is within the self-boundary. The hallucination (extrojection) is experienced phenomenologically as "not mine." It is outside the self-boundary.

The Person-Centered approach. The split between person and hallucination can be described in Client-Centered terms as "maximum incongruence between self and experience." The "fully functioning person" (Rogers, 1989), on the other hand, can be described as a "maximum congruence between self and experience."

The hallucination can be understood as the polar opposite of the fully functioning person. The hallucinatory person is profoundly closed to self-experience; the fully functioning person is profoundly open to self-experience.

Schizophrenia. Viewing the hallucination as extrojected beyond the self-boundary, and as "maximum incongruence between self and experience" closely parallels Binswanger's view of schizophrenia as "the breaking apart of the consistency of natural experience into rigid alternatives" (Spiegelberg, 1972).

These multiple views converge to form a conception of schizophrenia as the profound rending of the self-structure. It also provides an understanding of the psychotherapy of schizophrenia as developing a cohesion of the self-structure.

The unconscious. Freud described the dream as the "royal road to the unconscious." However, I would describe the hallucination as a royal road to the unconscious. Why? The first reason lies in issues of clinical method. In terms of experiential presence, the hallucination is more here and now, whereas the dream was last night. The hallucination is current immediacy. It has more experiential presence and potency. Hallucinations are often three-dimensional, colored, well-lighted, and available for years. This leads to the second major significance for clinical method. Because of their continued recurrence, hallucinations are repeatedly accessible to daytime consciousness. Despite their psychotic nature, hallucinations are more accessible.

Their next value as an approach to the unconscious is their capability to directly process into what was not conscious. This seems to present more accuracy than an interpretation that is the therapist's formulation or metaphor.

Finally, the Pre-Symbol itself is a structure that is not conscious. The hallucination is a literal fragment of the unconscious.

NOTE

1. Pre-Symbolic Process II was originally named "Proto-Symbolic" method and was published by this author in 1977 in the *Journal of Mental Imagery, 1* (2, Fall), 339–42.

The term "Proto-Symbolic" originated with Szasz's conception of Protolanguage (Szasz, 1961). This author defined the Proto-Symbolic method as the reflecting techniques applied to the self-indicating, self-emotive, self-processing, and self-integrating stages of hallucinatory process.

The term "Protosymbol" was also used by G. Beneditti (1992), in "The Psychotherapy of Psychotic and Schizophrenic Patients and Factors Facilitating This," *USA-Europe Conference on Facilitating Climate for the Thera-*

peutic Relation in Mental Health Services (8th Perugia Meeting of Medicine and Psychiatry), Borri, P., R. Quartesan, and P. Moretti (eds.), Arp Perugia, Italy, pp. 14–15.

Beneditti writes:

We must live beside the patient within the paradox of accepting his reality and being unable to accept it; of reading his "symbols" for ourselves, but responding to them as *"protosymbols" able to be transformed, but not yet rationalized*. . . . By the term "Protosymbol," I mean to define a delusion, a hallucination, an abnormal experience which cannot yet be a symbol for the patient, but can constitute the germ of it literally, "protosymbol". . . . Putting it somewhat schematically, the protosymbol may be thus modified by using the method of *positivising progression*.

The hallucination is interpreted by means of the therapist's free association. The hallucination has become a therapeutic image, a transitional subject: "The protosymbol begets the symbol."

Part IV

CONCLUSION

Chapter 8

Afterthoughts and Future Possibilities

AFTERTHOUGHTS

Gestalt Theory

Some leading Client-Centered therapists (Tausch, 1988) suggest integration with other theoretical orientations. In this book there are three such attempts involving the Gestalt approach.

First, in Chapter 5, Pre-Therapy acknowledges the influence of Fritz Perls' concept of contact as an ego function. Perls did not elaborate the meaning of this concept; thus, Pre-Therapy evolved the conceptions of reality, affective, and communicative contact. These formulations were then described theoretically as the contact functions.

The second attempt at fusion with the Gestalt approach occurs in Chapter 7. In Gestalt therapy, the dream is considered an aspect of self to be integrated. It is a parallel interpretation that the hallucination is a self-fragment to be integrated. This view is confirmed by Pre-Symbolic case studies.

The next point of theoretical integration concerns the language and concept of extrojection. I defined extrojection as the hallucination being experienced beyond the self-boundary. This language is consistent with the Gestalt tradition of what I call the "psychody-namics of experiencing": introjection, projection, retroflection, de-flection, and confluence (Frew, 1986).

The consequence of developing the concept of extrojection is that it points at the split between self and self-fragment. It amplifies the "psychic distance" not conveyed by Freud's concept of projec-tion. Freud's term does not differentiate between dream and hal-lucination.

I hope that these theoretical influences have been assimilated in a manner that does not alter the form or function of the Person-Centered/Experiential approach but, rather, strengthens its contri-butions.

Psychoanalysis

The hallucination is a mode of symbolization that embodies the positive, expressive thrust of the organism to signify experience. This primitive intentionality is foundational to the concept of self-intentionality. This "proactive" sense of symbols allows sharp comparison with the regressive conception of symbols developed by psychoanalysis (Freud, 1935; Jones, 1938).

The regressive interpretation of psychotic expression is also confronted by the concept of pre-expressive. In Chapter 6, case material is presented that describes psychotic expression as lat-ently coherent and reality-based meaningfulness. A regressive model simply lacks the capacity to illuminate this positive drive to realistic meaning.

FUTURE POSSIBILITIES

Pre-Therapy: A Psychiatric Ward Model

Van Werde (1993) describes the use of psychological contact as the central organizing concept for a psychiatric ward milieu that services the broad range of semi-acute to semi-chronic psychotic clients. As he states: "Contact, which is seen as antidote for psy-chotic alienation from which all residents suffer, is the key word of the whole approach."

He goes on to say: "The aim of such an approach is to restore the ineffective contact functions so that basic contact with reality, affect, and communication becomes possible again. This all happens within a Person-Centered framework."

Van Werde (1993) indicates that there can be a polarity between ward structure and individual psychotic process. He resolves this by the use of contact reflections. An example of this follows:

In a ward meeting, Chantel suddenly stands up, points at the window and says, "I see them moving again." I reflected, word for word, and also, her anxious facial expression. This intervention seems to anchor her. She looks around, becomes aware of the group again, sits down and we all can continue with the ward meeting. . . .

The group is relieved that she's with us again and that a possible psychotic episode doesn't automatically lead to repressive interaction, but instead is dealt with in a very accepting and containing manner.

Van Werde further relates: "In these meetings, we offer a great deal of opportunity to work with reality, affect, and communication, be it in this group setting. It is clear that we are not a psychotherapeutic group since processing of individual themes isn't done."

Another application of contact in the ward milieu concerns work therapy. Staff responses had usually been rather product-focused ("It looks good; when will this be ready?"). This was changed to a process-focused response that is consistent with the client's level of functioning: for example, "You're using a yellow pencil" (situational reflection). Another example would be, "You are drawing a face; yesterday you drew a face" (reiterative reflection). Still another example is "You look sad today" (facial reflection). Further, "You say it is difficult for you to sit there" (word-for-word reflection). Psychological space and contact with the patient are established, drawing them out of a non-responsive autistic world.

Contact was also utilized as a social work intervention. Schizophrenia was explained to parents as a contact impairment. Clients were described as having loss of contact with the world, self, or other.

Van Werde (1993) continues:

Basic in all this thinking about the translation of the contact paradigm into
the establishing of a Person-Centered milieu is that we try not to deny
psychosis, nor hide it, nor paternalize the client. We see psychotic behavior
as Pre-Expressive behavior. That means we see such behavior as a way of
expressing meanings that are there, but not yet fully in process, nor
available to the person.

Van Werde also describes the use of psychiatric medications.
He says:

Since we work in a medical hospital, medication is one of the treatment
ingredients. We try to promote the attitude of working with psychosis
as a Pre-Expressive structure. For reasons of a personal or ward-life
nature, we might propose that tranquilizers are used rather than the
very incisive neuroleptics. This is less inhibiting of the person's proactive forces.

He concludes by saying: "Frequently, progress translates itself
in an increased quality of life; a more 'being in contact' and more
living in the 'here and now.' In alliance with the strengthened
Contact Functions, maybe the therapist and client can approach
psychotherapy."
Van Werde's description of the ward milieu is certainly a genuine example of Pre-Therapy.

Pre-Therapy and "Voices"

During lectures concerning visual hallucinations, I have often
been asked about "voices." Generally, I have answered by indicat-
ing that my methods would be applicable. However, at that time,
there was no clinical evidence. The following is a recent vignette
that illustrates the use of contact reflections with audio hallucinations, in the context of a psychodrama session.

The client was a young woman who had previously lived in a
foreign country. At age 12 she was sexually abused. Her abusers
told her that if she disclosed the abuse, she and her family would
not be allowed to emigrate to the United States.

During the process of a psychodrama session at a mental health facility, the client reported hearing voices.

Client:	The voices. [Client puts hands on head.]
Therapist: BR	Your hands are on your head.
Client:	[Moves hands to cover her eyes.]
Therapist: FR	Your hands cover your eyes.
Therapist: BR	You're breathing deeply.
Client:	[The client removes her hands from her eyes and looks at the floor.]
Therapist: SR	You're looking at the floor.
Therapist: SR	There is a green carpet in this room.
Client:	[No response.]
Therapist: SR	We're standing here together.
Therapist: BR	You're breathing easier now.
Client:	[The client looks directly at the therapist.]
Therapist: SR	You looked directly at me.
Client:	[The client puts her hands on the side of her head and then over her ears.] I hear voices.
Therapist: WWR	You hear voices.
Client:	The voice says, "You die, you should kill yourself."
Therapist: WWR	The voice says, "You die. You should kill yourself."

Looking directly at the therapist, the client began her story about the actual abuse scene. Reality contact had been established.

Therapist: RR	You said earlier that you heard voices.

Communicative contact about the voices had been developed by the use of Pre-Therapy. The therapist then changed to classical psychodramatic technique, that is, developing the roles for the drama and setting the scene.

Therapist:	Is it one voice or many?
Client:	One.
Therapist:	Male or female?
Client:	Male. . . . My brother.
Therapist:	Choose someone in the group to be your brother.

The therapist states:

Further evidence for Reality Contact is indicated by the client's ability to choose a group member to be in the role of her brother. As the psycho-drama continued, the client was able to release her rage at her brother for his inability to protect her during the abuse. In addition, the client was able to process the guilt and anger over these feelings. These feelings were the origin of the voice: "You should die, you should kill yourself."

This vignette illustrates the use of voices as a therapeutic access, and the use of Pre-Therapy as an adjunctive method of contact to enable therapy.

Pre-Therapy for the Profoundly Retarded

Profoundly retarded clients are often severely impaired in terms of their social and communicative capacities. Contact re-flections have been used as a form of recreational social develop-ment for these clients. A pre-vocational workshop reports this application:

The counselor is trained in the use of the contact reflections; it is combined with *a playful attitude*. The counselor "plays" contactfully with the pro-foundly retarded during scheduled recreation times. The overt purpose is "play" and "entertainment." The clients learn to enjoy themselves through such a form of human contact. . . .
A further evolution of this recreational aspect of Pre-Therapy can be carried into the home so that parents may have more human contact with their profoundly retarded children. Again, it is taught to the parent as a form of "play," but obviously it is a form of *human* bonding or relationship building. Parents report that this diminishes the isolation of both parties with each other. This is especially true with non-verbal clients.

Pre-Therapy and Social Autism

Pre-Therapy can be applied to additional populations. At the suggestion of Dr. Henriette Morato of the University of Sao Paulo, Brazil, Pre-Therapy may have relevance for children who are cul-turally deprived or "socially autistic." These children have lost contact due to psychological trauma associated with severe poverty. As indigenous populations migrate to populated urban areas, family disorganization and family stress occur. This results in loss of self-sense and withdrawal from others, as well as withdrawal from reality itself. These are the "beggar children" of Sao Paulo.

References

Arieti, S. (1955). *Interpretation of Schizophrenia*. New York: Robert Brunner.

Badelt, I. (1990). Client-centered psychotherapy with mentally handicapped adults. In G. Lietaer, J. Rombauts, & R. Van Balen (Eds.), *Client-Centered and Experiential Psychotherapy in the Nineties* (pp. 671–681). Leuven, Belgium: Leuven University Press.

Berger, D. M. (1987). *Clinical Empathy*. Northvale, N.J.: Jason Aronson.

Binswanger, L. (1958). The existential analysis school of thought. *Existence: A New Dimension in Psychiatry and Psychology* (p. 194). New York: Basic Books.

Boss, M. (1963). A patient who taught the author to see and think differently. *Psychoanalysis and Daseinsanalysis.* (pp. 5–27). New York: Basic Books.

_____. (1980). Personal communication.

Brodley, B. (1990). Client-centered and experiential: Two different therapies. In G. Lietaer, J. Rombauts, & R. Van Balen (Eds.), *Client-Centered and Experiential Psychotherapy in the Nineties* (pp. 87–107). Leuven, Belgium: Leuven University Press.

Buber, M. (1964). Elements of the interhuman. In Friedman (Ed.), *The Worlds of Existentialism* (pp. 229, 547). New York: Random House.

Burton, A. (1973). The presentation of the face in psychotherapy. *Psychotherapy, Theory and Research, 10*(4), 301.

Cassirer, E. (1955). Man: An animal symbolicum. In D. Runes (Ed.), *Treasury of Philosophy* (pp. 227–29). New York: Philosophical Library.

Christensen, L. B. (1991). *Experimental Methodology*, 5th edn. Boston: Allyn and Bacon.

Cohen, J. (1968). Weighted kappa: Nominal scale agreement with provision for scaled disagreement or partial credit. *Psychological Bulletin*, 70, 213–20.

De Vre, R. (1992). *Prouty's pre-therapié*. Master's Thesis. Ghent, Belgium: Department of Psychology, University of Ghent.

Don, N. (1977). The transformation of conscious experience and its EEG correlates. *Journal of Altered States of Consciousness*, 3(2), 147–68.

Dosen, A. (1983). Autism and disturbances of social contact in mentally retarded children. Vienna, Austria: Paper presented to the VII World Congress of Psychiatry.

Farber, M. (1959). Consciousness and natural reality. *Naturalism and Subjectivism*, p. 87. Albany, NY: State University of New York Press.

――――. (1967). Descriptive philosophy. *Phenomenology and Existence: Toward a Philosophy within Nature*, (pp. 14–37). New York: Harper Torchbooks.

Freud, S. (1935). *A General Introduction to Psychoanalysis*. New York: Liverwright Co.

Frew, J. E. The functions and patterns of occurrence of individual contact styles during the developmental phases of the Gestalt group. *The Gestalt Journal*, Spring 1986, pp. 55–70.

Gendlin, E. T. (1964). A theory of personality change. In P. Worchel & D. Byrne (Eds.), *Personality Change* (pp. 102–48). New York: J. Wiley & Sons.

――――. (1968). The experiential response. In E. Hammer (Ed.), *Use of Interpretation in Treatment* (pp. 208–28). New York: Gruen and Stratton.

――――. (1969). Focusing. *Psychotherapy: Theory, Research and Practice*, 6(1), 4–15.

――――. (1970). Research in psychotherapy with schizophrenic patients and the nature of that "illness." In J. T. Hart & T. M. Tomlinson (Eds.), *New Directions in Client-Centered Therapy* (p. 288). Boston: Houghton Mifflin Co.

――――. (1973). Experiential psychotherapy. In R. Corsini (Ed.), *Current Psychotherapies* (pp. 317–52). Itasca, Ill.: F. E. Peacock Publishers.

――――. (1974). Client-centered and experiential psychotherapy. In D. Wexler & L. Rice (Eds.), *Innovations in Client-Centered Therapy* (pp. 211–16). New York: J. Wiley & Sons.

――――. (1978). *Focusing*. New York: Everest House.

_____. (1979). Experiential psychotherapy. In R. Corsini (Ed.), *Current Psychotherapies*, 2nd edn. (pp. 340–73). Itasca, Ill.: F. E. Peacock Publishers.

_____. (1981). *Focusing*, rev. edn. New York: Bantam Books.

_____. (1986). *Let Your Body Interpret Your Dreams*. Wilmette, Ill.: Chiron Publications.

Gendlin, E. T., & Berlin, J. (1961). Galvanic skin response correlates: Different modes of experiencing. *Journal of Clinical Psychology, 17*, 73–77.

Gurswitch, A. Gelb-Goldstein's concept of concrete and categorical attitude and the phenomenology of ideation. In J. Wild (Ed.), *Studies in Phenomenology and Psychology* (pp. 359–89). Evanston, Ill.: Northwestern University Press.

Hart, J. T. (1970). The development of client-centered therapy. In J. T. Hart & T. M. Tomlinson (Eds.), *New Directions in Client-Centered Therapy* (pp. 3–22). Boston: Houghton Mifflin Co.

Havens, L. (1962). The placement and movement of hallucinations in space, phenomenology and theory. *International Journal of Psychoanalysis, 43*, 426–35.

Hendricks, M. (1986). Experiencing level as a therapeutic variable. *Person-Centered Review 1*(2), 141–62.

Jaspers, K., (1971). *Philosophy*, Vol. 3. Chicago: University of Chicago Press.

Jones, E. (1938). The theory of symbolism. *Papers on Psychoanalysis* (p. 183). Baltimore: W. Wood and Co.

Karon, B., & Vanderbos, G. (1981). *Psychotherapy of Schizophrenia*. New York: Aaronson.

Laing, R. D. (1990). Minkowski and schizophrenia. In K. Hoeller (Ed.), *Readings in Existential Psychology and Psychiatry*. (Special issue of *Review of Existential Psychology and Psychiatry*.) Seattle, Wash.: 195–98.

Langer, S. K. (1961). *Philosophy in a New Key*. New York: Mentor Books.

Leijssen, M., & Roelens, L. (1988). Herstel Van Contactfuncties Bij Zwaar Gestoorde Patienten Door Middel Van Prouty's Pre-Therapie (The contact functions of Prouty's Pre-Therapy) (pp. 21–34). Belgium: *Tijdschrift Klinische Psychologie*.

Maher, A. (1992). Discovery oriented psychotherapy research: Rationale, aims and methods. In R. B. Miller (Ed.), *The Restoration of Dialogue: Readings in the Philosophy of Clinical Psychology* (pp. 570–84). Washington, D.C.: American Psychological Association.

Makkreel, R. A. (1986). Dilthey and universal hermeneutics: The status of the human sciences. In S. Glynn (Ed.), European Philosophy and the Human Sciences (p. 3). Hampshire, England, Gower Publishing.

Mallin, S. B. (1979). *Merleau-Ponty's Philosophy*. New Haven, Conn.: Yale University Press.

Maurer-Groeli, Y. A. (1976). Korperzentrierte Gruppenpsychotherapie bei akut schizophren Erkrankten *Arch. Psychiat. Nervenkr. 221*, 259–71.

Mearns, D., & Thorne, B. (1990). *Person-Centered Counselling in Action*. London: Sage Publications.

Merleau-Ponty, M. (1962). The phenomenal field. In T. Honderich (Ed.), *The Phenomenology of Perception* (p. 60). London: Routledge and Kegan Paul.

Minkowski, E. (1970). Schizophrenia. In J. Wild (Ed.), *Lived Time* (pp. 281–82). Evanston, Ill.: Northwestern University Press.

Perls, F. S. (1969). The ego as a function of the organism. *Ego, Hunger and Aggression* (p. 139). New York: Vintage Books.

———. (1976). *The Gestalt Approach and Eyewitness to Therapy*. New York: Bantam Edition.

Peters, H. (1981). *Luisterend Helpen: Poging Tot een Beter Omgaan Met de Zwakzinnige Medemes*. Lochem/Gent, Netherlands: De Tijdstroom.

———. (1986a). Client-Centered Benaderingswijzen in de Zwakzinningenzorg. In R. Van Balen, M. Leijssen, & G. Lietaer (Eds.), *Droom en Werkelijkheid* (pp. 205–20). Belgium: Acco Press.

———. (1986b). Prouty's pré-therapie methode en de behandeling van hallucinaties een verslag (Prouty's Pre-Therapy methods and the treatment of hallucinations) (pp. 26–34). Netherlands: RUIT (Maart).

———. (1992). *Psychotherapie Bij Geestelijk Gehandicapten*. Amsterdam: Swets and Zeitlinger.

Polster, E., & Polster, M. (1974). *Gestalt Therapy Integrated*. New York: Vintage Books.

Portner, M. Client-centered therapy with mentally retarded persons: Catherine and Ruth. In G. Lietaer, J. Rombauts, & R. Van Balen (Eds.), *Client-Centered and Experiential Psychotherapy in the Nineties* (pp. 559–69). Leuven, Belgium: Leuven University Press.

Prouty, G. (1966). Unpublished tape recording: *Psychotherapy with a Psychotic Retardate*. Recorded at the Lt. J. P. Kennedy School for Exceptional Children, Palos Park, Ill.

———. (1976). Pre-therapy, a method of treating pre-expressive psychotic and retarded patients. *Psychotherapy: Theory, Research and Practice, 13*(Fall), 290–94.

_____ . (1977). Protosymbolic method: A phenomenological treatment of schizophrenic hallucinations. *Journal of Mental Imagery*, 1(2 Fall), 339–42.

_____ . (1983). Hallucinatory contact: A phenomenological treatment of schizophrenics. *Journal of Communication Therapy*, 2(1), 99–103.

_____ . (1985). The development of reality, affect and communication in psychotic retardates. Unpublished manuscript.

_____ . (1986). The pre-symbolic structure and therapeutic transformation of hallucinations. In M. Wolpin, J. Shorr & L. Kreuger (Eds.), *Imagery*, Vol. 4 (pp. 99–106). New York: Plenum Press.

_____ . (1990). Pre-therapy: A theoretical evolution in the person-centered/experiential psychotherapy of schizophrenia and retardation. In G. Lietaer, J. Rombauts, & R. Van Balen (Eds.), *Client-Centered and Experiential Psychotherapy in the Nineties* (pp. 645–58). Leuven, Belgium: Leuven University Press.

_____ . (1991). The pre-symbolic structure and processing of schizophrenic hallucinations: The problematic of a non-process structure. In Lois Fusek (Ed.), *New Directions in Client-Centered Therapy: Practice with Difficult Client Populations* (pp. 1–18). Chicago: Chicago Counseling and Psychotherapy Research Center.

_____ . (1992). Mental health lectures. Chicago Heights, Ill.: Prairie State College.

Prouty, G., & Cronwall, M. (1990). Psychotherapy with a depressed mentally retarded adult: An application of pre-therapy. In A. Dosen & F. Menolascino (Eds.), *Depression in Mentally Retarded Children and Adults* (pp. 281–93). Leiden, Netherlands: Logan Publications.

Prouty, G., & Kubiak, M. (1988a). The development of communicative contact with a catatonic schizophrenic. *Journal of Communication Therapy*, 4(1), 13–20.

_____ . (1988b). Pre-therapy with mentally retarded/psychotic clients. *Psychiatric Aspects of Mental Retardation Reviews*, 7(10), 62–66.

Prouty, G., & Pietrzak, S. (1988). Pre-therapy method applied to persons experiencing hallucinatory images. *Person-Centered Review*, 3(4), 426–41.

Riepe, D. (1973). Marvin Farber and the program of naturalistic phenomenology. *Phenomenology and Natural Existence* (pp. 26–48). Albany: State University of New York Press.

Rogers, C. (1942). *Counseling and Psychotherapy*. Boston: Houghton Mifflin Co.

_____ . (1957). The necessary and sufficient conditions of therapeutic personality change. *Journal of Consulting Psychology*, 21(2), 95–103.

———. (1959). A theory of therapy, personality and interpersonal relationships as developed in the client-centered framework. In E. Koch (Ed.), *Psychology: A Study of a Science*, Vol. 3 (p. 251). New York: McGraw-Hill.

———. (1961). A process conception of psychotherapy. *On Becoming a Person* (pp. 125–59). Boston: Houghton Mifflin.

———. (1963). The actualizing tendency in relation to "motives" and to consciousness. In M. Jones (Ed.), *Nebraska Symposium on Motivation* (pp. 1–24). Lincoln, Neb.: University of Nebraska Press.

———. (1966). Client-centered therapy. In S. Arieti (Ed.), *American Handbook of Psychiatry*, Vol. 3 (p. 104). New York: Basic Books.

———. (1975). Empathic: An unappreciated way of being. *The Counseling Psychologist*, 5(2), 2–10.

———. (1977). *Carl Rogers on Personal Power: Inner Strength and Its Revolutionary Impact*. London: Constable and Co.

———. (1978). The formative tendency. *Journal of Humanistic Psychology*, 18, 23–26.

———. (1989). A therapist view of the good life: The fully functioning person. In H. Kirschenbaum (Ed.). *The Carl Rogers Reader* (pp. 409–20). Boston, Mass.: Houghton Mifflin.

Rogers, C., Gendlin, E. T., Kiesler, D. J., & Truax, C. B. (1967). The findings in brief. In C. Rogers (Ed.), *The Therapeutic Relationship and Its Impact: A Study of Psychotherapy with Schizophrenics* (pp. 73–93). Madison, Wis.: University of Wisconsin Press.

Roy, Barbara C. (1991). A client-centered approach to multiple personality and dissociative process. In L. Fusek (Ed.), *New Directions in Client-Centered Therapy: Practice with Difficult Client Populations* (pp. 18–40). Chicago: Chicago Counseling and Psychotherapy Research Center.

Ruederich, S., & Menolascino, F. (1984). Dual diagnosis of mental retardation: An overview. In F. Menolascino & J. Stark (Eds.), *Handbook of Mental Illness in the Mentally Retarded* (p. 70). New York: Plenum Press.

Rychlak, J. (1971). Applied phenomenology: The client-centered psychology of Carl Rogers. *Introduction To Personality and Psychotherapy* (p. 410). Boston: Houghton Mifflin.

Sarbin, T. R., & Juhass, J. (1967). The historical background of the concept of hallucinations. *Journal of the History of Behavioral Sciences*, 4(3), 339–58.

Sartre, J. P. (1956). *Being and Nothingness*. New York: Washington Square Press.

Sasche, R. (1990). Acting purposefully in client-centered therapy. In J. Drenth, J. Sergeant, & R. Takens (Eds.), *European Perspectives in*

Psychology, Vol. 2 (pp. 65–79). West Essex, England: Wiley & Son.

Scheler, M. (1953). Phenomenology and the theory of cognition. *Selected Philosophical Essays.* Evanston, Ill.: Northwestern University Press.

Sovner, R., & Hurley, A. (1983). Do the mentally retarded suffer from affective illness? *Archives of General Psychiatry, 40,* 61–67.

Spiegelberg, H. (1972). Phenomenology in psychology and psychiatry. In J. Wild (Ed.). *Northwestern University Studies in Phenomenology and Existential Philosophy* (p. 226). Evanston, Ill.: Northwestern University Press.

——— . (1978). The pure phenomenology of Edmund Husserl. *The Phenomenological Movement: A Historical Introduction,* Vol. 1, 2nd edn. (p. 107). Boston: Martinus Nijhoff, 1978.

Spinelli, E. (1989). *The Interpreted World: An Introduction to Phenomenological Psychology.* London: Sage Publications.

Stikkers, K. W. (1985). Phenomenology as psychic technique of non-resistance. In W. Hamrick (Ed.), *Phenomenology in Practice and Theory* (pp. 129–52). London: Martinus Nijhoff, Dordrecht.

Szasz, T. S. (1961). *The Myth of Mental Illness: Foundations of a Theory of Personal Conduct.* New York: Paul B. Hoeber.

Tausch, R. (1988). The supplementation of client-centered communication-therapy with other validated therapeutic methods: A client-centered necessity. Hamburg, Germany: Psychologisches Institut III, University of Hamburg. Plenary address, International Conference on Client-Centered and Experiential Psychotherapy, University Leuven/Belgium, September 12–16.

Van Balen, R. (1991). On Rogers' and Gendlin's theory of personality change. Private circulation. Stirling, Scotland: *2nd International Conference on Person-Centered/Experiential Psychotherapy* (pp. 8–17).

Van Belle, H. (1980). *Basic Intent and Therapeutic Approach of Carl R. Rogers.* Toronto, Canada: Wedge Publishing Foundation.

Van Werde, D. (1990). Psychotherapy with a retarded schizo-affective woman: An application of Prouty's pre-therapy. In A. Dosen, A. Van Gennep, & G. Zwanikken (Eds.), *Treatment of Mental Illness and Behavioral Disorder in the Mentally Retarded: Proceedings of International Congress, May 3rd and 4th, Amsterdam, The Netherlands* (pp. 469–77). Leiden, The Netherlands: Logon Publications.

——— . (1993). *The Translation of the Contact-Paradigm into a Ward-Approach.* Personal communication.

Warner, M. S. (1991). Fragile process. In L. Fusek (Ed.), *New Directions in Client-Centered Therapy: Practice with Difficult Client Populations* (pp. 41–58). Chicago: Chicago Counseling and Psychotherapy Research Center.

Watson, N. (1984). The empirical status of Rogers' hypotheses of the necessary and sufficient conditions for effective psychotherapy. In R. Levant & J. Shlien (Eds.), *Client-Centered Therapy and the Person-Centered Approach* (pp. 17–40). New York: Praeger.

Whitehead, A. N. (1927). *Symbolism.* New York: Capricorn Books.

Zimring, F., & Raskin, N. (1992). Carl Rogers and client/person-centered therapy. In D. Freedman (Ed.), *History of Psychotherapy: A Century of Change* (pp. 629–56). Washington, D.C.: American Psychological Association.

Zucconi, A. (1984). Stress intervention for helping professionals. In A. Segrera (Ed.), *Proceedings of the First International Forum of the Person-Centered Approach.* Oaxtepec Morelos, Mexico: University Ibero Americana.

Index

About the Author

GARRY PROUTY is Professor of Psychology and Mental Health at Prairie State College. He is also a Faculty Associate of the Nisonger Center at Ohio State University and a member of the Clinical Advisory Committee for the Chicago Counseling and Psychotherapy Center. He serves as an editorial consultant to the *Person-Centered Journal* and is the author of a chapter in the forthcoming *Handbook of Treatment of Mental Illness and Behavior Disorders in Children and Adults with Mental Retardation.*

ISBN 0-275-94543-X

90000>

EAN

9 780275 945435

HARDCOVER BAR CODE